Collins

11+ Maths

Quick Practice Tests
Ages 10-11
Book 3

Anne Stothers

Contents

About this book 3	Test 12 37
Test 1 4	Test 13 40
Test 2 7	Test 14 43
Test 3 10	Test 15 46
Test 4 13	Test 16 49
Test 5 16	Test 17 52
Test 6 19	Test 18 55
Test 7 22	Test 19 58
Test 8 25	Test 20 61
Test 9 28	Test 21 64
Test 10 31	Test 22 67
Test 11 34	Answers 71

ACKNOWLEDGEMENTS

The author and publisher are grateful to the copyright holders for permission to use quoted materials and images.

Every effort has been made to trace copyright holders and obtain their permission for the use of copyright material. The author and publisher will gladly receive information enabling them to rectify any error or omission in subsequent editions. All facts are correct at time of going to press.

Published by Collins
An imprint of HarperCollins*Publishers* Limited
1 London Bridge Street
London SE1 9GF

HarperCollins*Publishers*
Macken House, 39/40 Mayor Street Upper,
Dublin 1, D01 C9W8, Ireland

ISBN: 978-0-00-876049-6

First published 2025

10 9 8 7 6 5 4 3 2 1

© HarperCollins*Publishers* Limited 2025

All rights reserved. No part of this publication may be reproduced, stored in a retrieval system, or transmitted, in any form or by any means, electronic, mechanical, photocopying, recording or otherwise, without the prior permission of Collins.

Without limiting the exclusive rights of any author, contributor or the publisher of this publication, any unauthorised use of this publication to train generative artificial intelligence (AI) technologies is expressly prohibited. HarperCollins also exercise their rights under Article 4(3) of the Digital Single Market Directive 2019/790 and expressly reserve this publication from the text and data mining exception.

British Library Cataloguing in Publication Data.

A CIP record of this book is available from the British Library.

Author: Anne Stothers
Publisher: Clare Souza
Project Manager and Editor: Richard Toms
Cover Design: Sarah Duxbury
Text and Page Design: Ian Wrigley
Layout and Artwork: Q2A Media
Production: Bethany Brohm
Printed in the United Kingdom

About this book

Familiarisation with 11+ test-style questions is a critical step in preparing your child for the 11+ selection tests. This book gives children lots of opportunities to test themselves in short, manageable bursts, helping to build confidence and improve the chance of test success.

It contains 22 tests designed to develop key numeracy skills. An example question and answer can be found at the start of Test 1.

- Each test is designed to be completed within a short amount of time. Frequent, short bursts of revision are found to be more productive than lengthier sessions.

- GL Assessment tests can be quite time-pressured so these practice tests will help your child become accustomed to this style of questioning.

- We recommend your child uses a pencil to complete the tests, so that they can rub out the answers and try again at a later date if necessary.

- Your child will need a pencil and a rubber to complete the tests as well as some spare paper for rough working. They will also need to be able to see a clock/watch and should have a quiet place in which to do the tests.

- Your child should **not** use a calculator for any of these tests.

- Answers to every question are provided at the back of the book, with explanations given where appropriate.

- After completing the tests, your child should revisit their weaker areas and attempt to improve their scores and timings.

For more information about 11+ preparation and other practice resources available from Collins, go to our website at:

collins.co.uk/11plus

Test 1

You have 10 minutes to complete this test.

You have 10 questions to complete within the given time.

Circle the letter above the correct answer.

EXAMPLE

Which number should go in the box?

$$93.6 \div \boxed{} = 0.0936$$

A	B	Ⓒ	D	E
10	100	1000	10000	100000

① Work out 16 × 29

A	B	C	D	E
444	203	364	464	454

② A rectangle has a perimeter of 20 cm.

Which of the answers below **cannot** be the correct dimensions of the rectangle?

A	B	C	D	E
2 cm and 8 cm	1 cm and 9 cm	3 cm and 7 cm	4 cm and 5 cm	6 cm and 4 cm

③ Which metric units would be most suitable for measuring the amount of water in a glass?

A	B	C	D	E
cm	mm	ml	L	m

④ Use the graph to convert 90 litres to gallons.

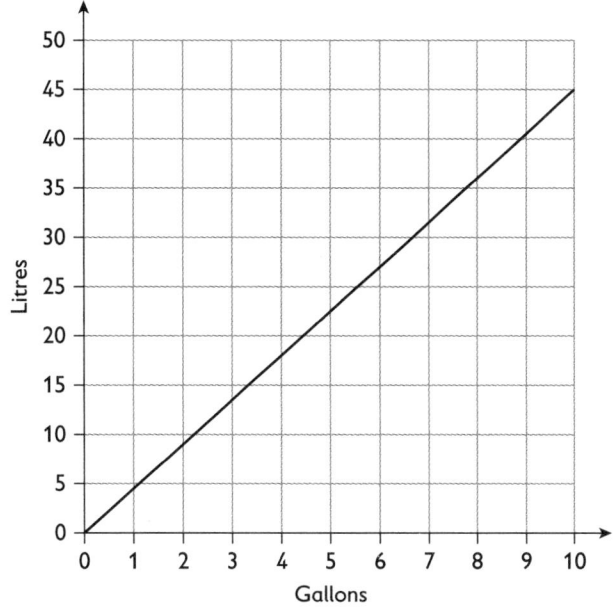

A	B	C	D	E
18 gallons	20 gallons	10 gallons	405 gallons	450 gallons

⑤ Theo buys a tea, two coffees and a cake from this menu.

Menu

Tea £2.40
Coffee £3.25
Cake £2.95
Scone £3.50

How much change should Theo receive from a £20 note?

A	B	C	D	E
£8.15	£9	£11.85	£8.60	£11.40

⑥ Which number is 17 less than −9?

A	B	C	D	E
8	−8	−26	26	−17

7) Isla has a jar of 300 sweets.

She gives $\frac{1}{3}$ of the sweets to Adam.

She then gives $\frac{2}{5}$ of the remaining sweets to Leo.

How many sweets does Isla have left?

A	B	C	D	E
120	80	200	90	100

8) Work out the size of angle x.

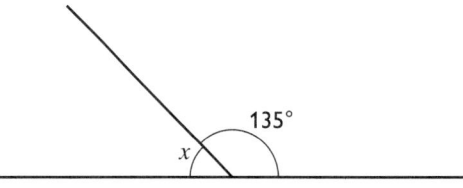

A	B	C	D	E
145°	225°	55°	35°	45°

9) Louis is thinking of two numbers.

Both numbers are greater than 1.

The sum of the squares of the numbers is 100.

What are the two numbers?

A	B	C	D	E
3 and 4	6 and 8	5 and 6	7 and 8	3 and 9

10) What is the name of this shape?

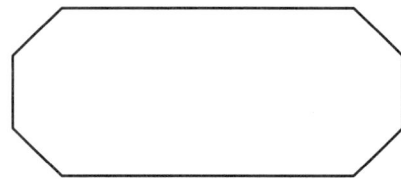

A	B	C	D	E
Octagon	Hexagon	Trapezium	Heptagon	Pentagon

Score: ………… / 10

Test 2

You have **10 minutes** to complete this test.

You have **10 questions** to complete within the given time.

Circle the letter above the correct answer.

1) Sal puts counters into bags.

   He has 167 counters and puts 13 counters into each bag.

   How many bags can he completely fill?

A	B	C	D	E
11	12	13	14	15

2) How many faces does a cuboid have?

A	B	C	D	E
4	5	6	7	8

3) A pair of jeans normally costs £48.

   In a sale, there is $\frac{1}{3}$ off the normal price.

   Work out the cost of the pair of jeans in the sale.

A	B	C	D	E
£16	£32	£24	£36	£34

4) Here are the first five terms in a sequence:

   −3   1   5   9   13

   What is the 10th term in the sequence?

A	B	C	D	E
33	23	40	25	29

Questions continue on next page

5) Here are some cards from a game.

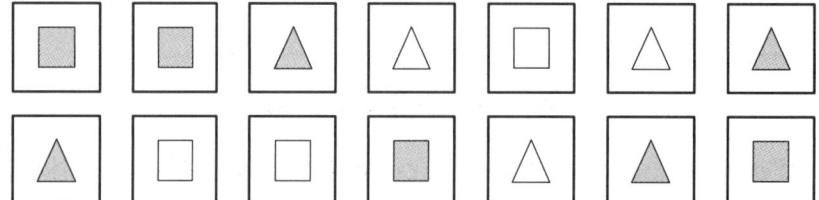

Kai picks a card at random.

What is the probability that he picks a white triangle?

A	B	C	D	E
$\frac{4}{14}$	$\frac{7}{14}$	$\frac{2}{14}$	$\frac{3}{14}$	$\frac{3}{7}$

6) What are these measurements in order of size, smallest first?

400 cm   2 m   0.003 km   2500 mm

A	B	C	D	E
400 cm, 0.003 km, 2500 mm, 2 m	2500 mm, 2 m, 0.003 km, 400 cm	2 m, 2500 mm, 400 cm, 0.003 km	2500 mm, 400 cm, 2 m, 0.003 km	2 m, 2500 mm, 0.003 km, 400 cm

7) Ava buys 5 pens and 9 rulers for £7.85

Each pen costs 85p.

Work out the cost of each ruler.

A	B	C	D	E
25p	30p	35p	40p	45p

8) The pie chart shows the colours of 48 balloons at a party.

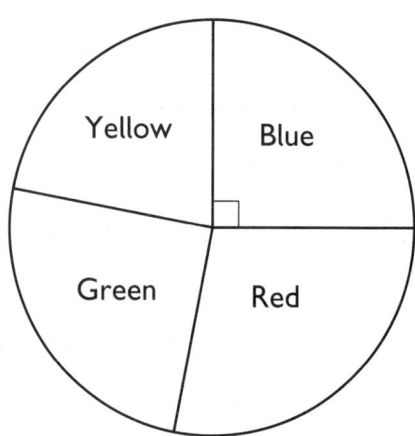

How many balloons are **not** blue?

A	B	C	D	E
12	24	36	16	30

9 At a party, guests can have either ice cream, cake or both.

The Venn diagram shows the choices the guests made.

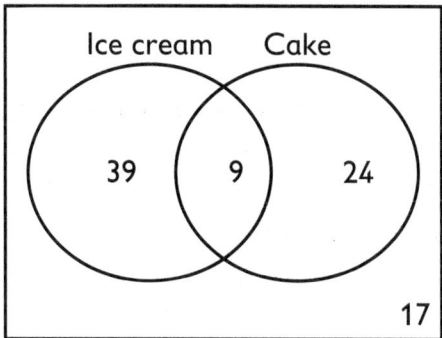

How many guests were at the party?

A	B	C	D	E
89	72	98	63	80

10 Decrease £80 by 20%

A	B	C	D	E
£60	£106	£72	£62	£64

Score: ………… / 10

Test 3

You have **10 minutes** to complete this test.

You have **10 questions** to complete within the given time.

Circle the letter above the correct answer.

1) What is this number written in digits?

Three hundred and two thousand, seven hundred and six

A	B	C	D	E
320 706	302 760	302 706	302 076	320 076

2) Work out $-5 + 7 \times 2$

A	B	C	D	E
9	−9	4	−4	24

3) What is the missing number in this sequence?

−1   ☐   17   26

A	B	C	D	E
6	7	8	9	10

4) Work out the difference between the largest and smallest possible numbers that can be made from all four of the following digits.

6   1   3   7

A	B	C	D	E
6255	6237	5976	5346	6264

10

5 A tree was 3.2 m tall.

It grew another 90 cm.

How tall in metres was the tree after it grew?

A	B	C	D	E
3.29 m	4.1 m	4.01 m	12.2 m	93.2 m

6 The pictogram shows the number of traffic cones placed on three roads.

There were 15 more traffic cones placed on East Street than on North Road.

North Road	△
East Street	△ △ △ △
South Avenue	△ △

How many traffic cones were placed on South Avenue?

A	B	C	D	E
3	6	9	12	15

7 Which of these shapes is **not** a quadrilateral?

A	B	C	D	E

Questions continue on next page

11

(8) In its simplest form, what fraction of the shape below is **not** shaded?

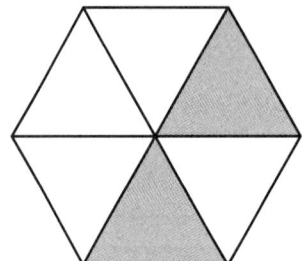

A	B	C	D	E
$\frac{1}{2}$	$\frac{1}{3}$	$\frac{4}{6}$	$\frac{2}{4}$	$\frac{2}{3}$

(9) Cara thought of a number.

She divided it by 2, then subtracted 6, and squared the result.

The final answer was 16.

Which number did Cara think of?

A	B	C	D	E
4	8	10	20	40

(10) Solve $2a - 7 = 21$

A	B	C	D	E
$a = 7$	$a = 2$	$a = 13$	$a = 14$	$a = 9$

Test 4

You have 10 minutes to complete this test.

You have 10 questions to complete within the given time.

Circle the letter above the correct answer.

1. What is $\frac{5}{13}$ of 52?

A	B	C	D	E
5	13	20	21	24

2. Each edge of the cube below has a length of 4 cm.

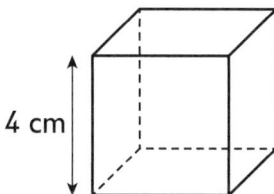

What is the surface area of the cube?

A	B	C	D	E
8 cm²	20 cm²	64 cm²	96 cm²	120 cm²

3. Which number is 6700 smaller than three hundred thousand?

A	B	C	D	E
299 330	293 300	29 330	2 993 300	293 330

Questions continue on next page

13

(4) Jo saves £21.50 per week.

How many weeks will it take Jo to save £172?

A	B	C	D	E
5	6	7	8	9

(5) A bus leaves a station at 11.45 am and arrives at its destination at 12.32 pm.

How long does the journey take?

A	B	C	D	E
47 minutes	37 minutes	43 minutes	53 minutes	57 minutes

(6) What percentage of £3 is 60p?

A	B	C	D	E
5%	2%	15%	50%	20%

(7) My teacher's age is:

a square number

a multiple of 3

less than 70.

How old is my teacher?

A	B	C	D	E
64	36	49	52	25

(8) Work out the value of $9^2 - \sqrt{49}$

A	B	C	D	E
25	11	32	74	75

9 Mo goes to a shop and buys the items listed on the receipt.

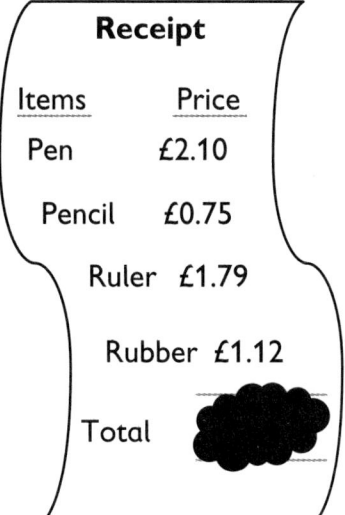

He pays with a £10 note.

How much change should he receive?

A	B	C	D	E
£5.24	£5.36	£4.33	£5.76	£4.24

10 Find the range of these fractions.

$$\frac{1}{2} \quad \frac{2}{3} \quad \frac{3}{4} \quad \frac{5}{12}$$

A	B	C	D	E
$\frac{1}{3}$	$\frac{1}{12}$	$\frac{1}{4}$	$\frac{1}{2}$	$\frac{1}{6}$

Score: .... / 10

Test 5

You have **10 minutes** to complete this test.

You have **10 questions** to complete within the given time.

Circle the letter above the correct answer.

① A bag contains 10 red counters and 13 blue counters.

Three blue counters are added to the bag.

In its simplest form, what is the new ratio of red counters to blue counters in the bag?

A	B	C	D	E
5 : 16	5 : 8	10 : 8	10 : 16	2 : 3

② What is $\frac{2}{3}$ of $\frac{1}{4}$ of 24?

A	B	C	D	E
2	3	4	5	6

③ A pizza is divided into 12 equal slices.

James eats 3 slices and Rachel eats 4 slices.

What fraction of the pizza is left?

A	B	C	D	E
$\frac{1}{12}$	$\frac{5}{12}$	$\frac{1}{2}$	$\frac{5}{6}$	$\frac{7}{12}$

④ A recipe requires 3 parts flour to 2 parts sugar.

If you use 12 cups of flour, how many cups of sugar do you need?

A	B	C	D	E
2	3	4	6	8

5) A square has sides of length 7 cm.

7 cm

Work out the perimeter of the square.

A	B	C	D	E
14 cm	49 cm	28 cm	21 cm	42 cm

6) A train leaves London at 14:45 and arrives at Derby at 16:20

How long does the journey last?

A	B	C	D	E
1 hour 20 minutes	1 hour 35 minutes	1 hour 45 minutes	2 hours	2 hours 35 minutes

7) Sarah has £5.50

She buys a pen for £1.25 and a notebook for £2.75

How much money does she have left?

A	B	C	D	E
£1.50	£1.75	£1.25	£2.00	£2.25

8) $x - 5 = 12$

What is the value of x?

A	B	C	D	E
7	60	2.4	17	19

Questions continue on next page

(9) Here are the scores of five students in a maths test:

56   63   71   78   82

Work out the mean score of the students.

A	B	C	D	E
70	72	75	76	78

(10) The bar chart shows the number of books read by four children — Ahmed, Brad, Chloe and Diana — over a period of five months.

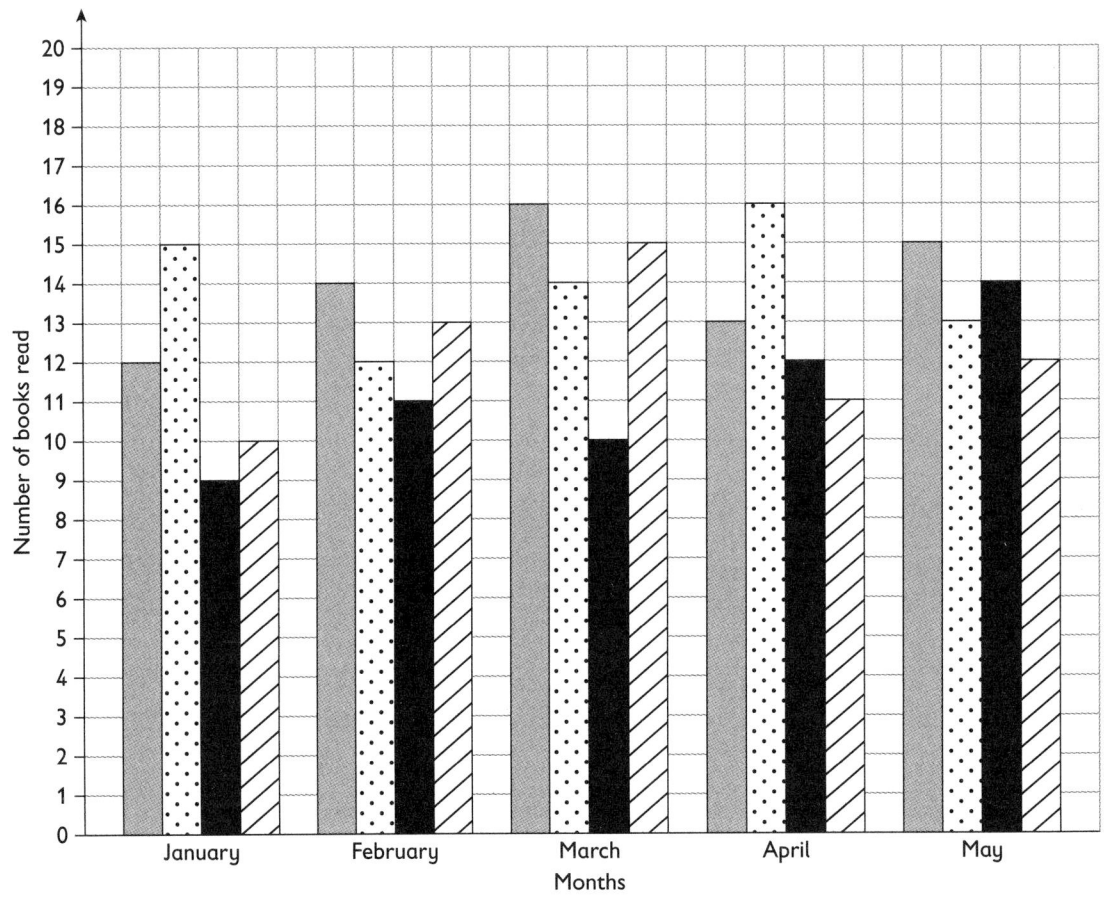

How many more books did the children read in the month that they read the most books compared with the month that they read the fewest books?

A	B	C	D	E
3	11	7	8	9

Score: ………… / 10

Test 6

You have 10 minutes to complete this test.

You have 10 questions to complete within the given time.

Circle the letter above the correct answer.

① Which arrow is pointing to 2.44?

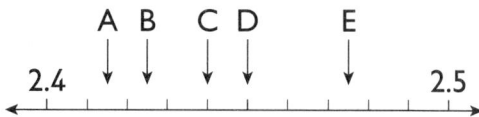

A	B	C	D	E
A	B	C	D	E

② The diagram shows a parallelogram.

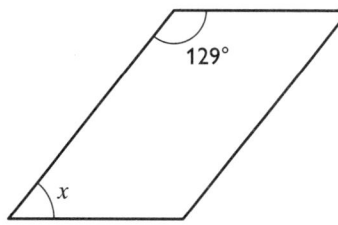

Work out the size of angle x.

A	B	C	D	E
231°	39°	49°	51°	129°

③ Which of these numbers is **not** a square number?

A	B	C	D	E
1	27	81	400	121

④ Here are the first five numbers in a sequence:

7   4   1   −2   −5

Which is the 10th number of the sequence?

A	B	C	D	E
−20	−18	−21	−23	−17

Questions continue on next page

5 The graph shows the total number of 'Good work stars' that a class earned over 10 weeks.

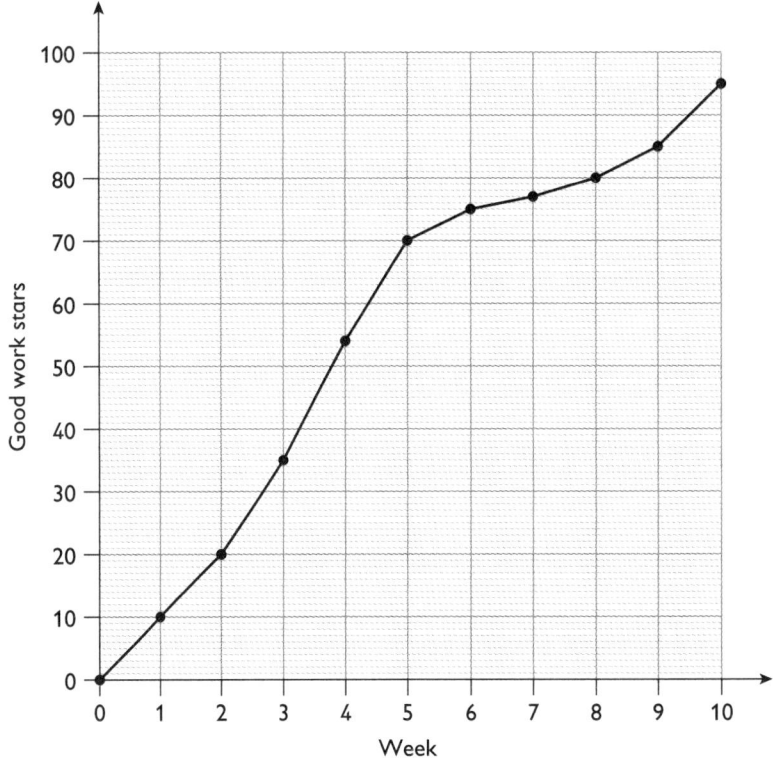

How many stars did the class earn during the fourth week?

A	B	C	D	E
10	6	11	23	19

6 Which of these numbers is **not** a factor of 80?

A	B	C	D	E
8	160	80	16	5

7 Charlie buys a scarf that normally costs £12.80

The price of the scarf is reduced by 10%

How much does Charlie pay for the scarf?

A	B	C	D	E
£11.52	£12.68	£12.00	£11.80	£11.20

8 One sheet of card has a thickness of 0.6 mm.

A pile of these sheets of card has a height of 48 cm.

How many sheets of card are in the pile?

A	B	C	D	E
0.08	0.8	8	80	800

9 Robyn spins this five-sided spinner two times.

Two sections of the spinner are labelled B, one section is labelled G, and two sections are labelled R. Each section is equal in size.

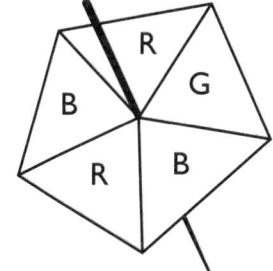

Which of these results is Robyn least likely to get?

A	B	C	D	E
Two Bs	Two Rs	Two Gs	One R and one B	One R and one G

10 A formula for converting miles (M) to kilometres (K) is $K = 1.6M$

Use the formula to convert 5 miles to kilometres.

A	B	C	D	E
5 km	8 km	6 km	10 km	7 km

Score: .... / 10

Test 7

You have 10 minutes to complete this test.

You have 10 questions to complete within the given time.

Circle the letter above the correct answer.

① At 6 am, the temperature was −4°C.

By 1 pm, the temperature had risen by 9°C.

What was the temperature at 1 pm?

A	B	C	D	E
−1°C	4°C	5°C	9°C	13°C

② Billy has 3.4 kilograms of rice.

He uses 500 grams of the rice.

How much rice does Billy have left in kilograms?

A	B	C	D	E
3.35 kg	290 kg	29 kg	2.9 kg	160 kg

③ A piece of ribbon is 240 cm long.

Petra cuts two 45 cm lengths off the ribbon.

She then cuts the rest of the ribbon into as many 40 cm lengths as possible.

Work out how many 40 cm lengths Petra cuts.

A	B	C	D	E
2	3	4	5	6

④ Work out the value of $(-3)^2$

A	B	C	D	E
6	−6	9	−9	3

(5) Work out the perimeter of this shape.

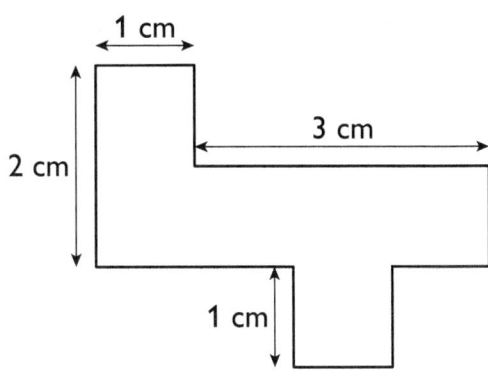

A	B	C	D	E
12 cm	13 cm	14 cm	15 cm	16 cm

(6) Which pair of numbers could be placed in the boxes below to make the fractions equivalent?

$$\frac{\square}{3} = \frac{12}{\square}$$

A	B	C	D	E
2 and 18	3 and 4	1 and 30	3 and 3	6 and 12

(7) A teacher asks some pupils how they travel to school.

The bar chart shows the results of the teacher's survey.

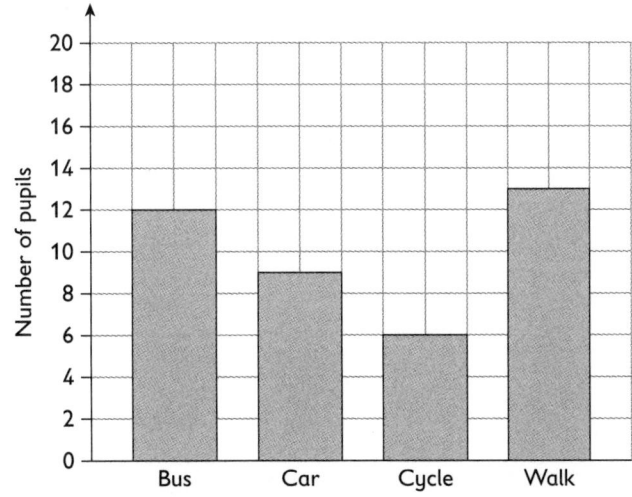

How many pupils did the teacher ask?

A	B	C	D	E
36	37	38	39	40

Questions continue on next page

8 Work out the range of the following numbers.

        6.4   2.3   9.01   0.23   7.6

A	B	C	D	E
4.1	1.2	6.71	7.37	8.78

9 Which number is exactly halfway between 7 and 14?

A	B	C	D	E
10	10.5	11	11.5	12

10 Tim drives a bus 38 weeks per year.

He drives an average of 307 miles each week.

Which is the best **estimate** for the total number of miles Tim drives the bus in one year?

A	B	C	D	E
1200	9000	90 000	12 000	16 000

Score: .... / 10

Test 8

You have 10 minutes to complete this test.

You have 10 questions to complete within the given time.

Circle the letter above the correct answer.

1. What is 506 709 rounded to the nearest thousand?

A	B	C	D	E
506 800	507 000	510 000	500 000	517 000

2. Fay collects china dolls.

   She has 12 shelves of china dolls.

   Each shelf has 27 china dolls.

   How many china dolls does Fay have in her collection altogether?

A	B	C	D	E
297	324	296	540	314

3. The numbers in the boxes form a sequence. Two numbers are missing.

   What are the missing numbers?

A	B	C	D	E
−11 and 9	−11 and 11	−9 and 11	−10 and 10	−9 and 10

4. Harry has 153 sweets. He shares them equally with his friends.

   Each person (including Harry) gets 17 sweets.

   How many friends did Harry share his sweets with?

A	B	C	D	E
5	6	7	8	9

Questions continue on next page

(5) Ravi wants to buy a pair of trainers which normally cost £120

The shop is offering a discount of 15% in a sale.

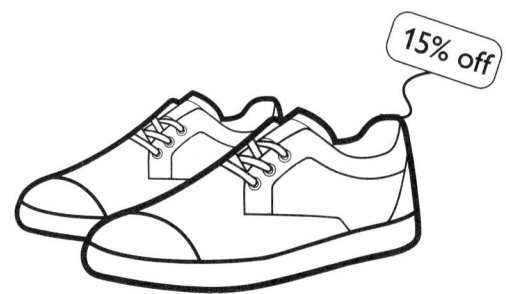

How much will Ravi save if he buys the trainers in the sale?

A	B	C	D	E
£102	£12	£24	£96	£18

(6) Which quadrilateral shape has one line of symmetry, two pairs of sides of equal length and one pair of diagonally opposite equal angles?

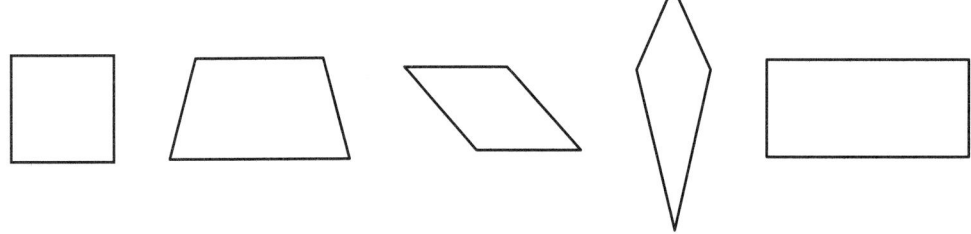

A	B	C	D	E
Square	Trapezium	Rhombus	Kite	Rectangle

(7) Paul buys four cakes costing £1.35 each and four identical drinks.

He pays with a £10 note.

He gets £2.20 change.

How much does Paul pay for each of the drinks?

A	B	C	D	E
£1.20	£2.40	80p	60p	40p

8 Rob thinks of a number.

He doubles the number and then adds 7 to get a total of 35

Which number did Rob think of?

A	B	C	D	E
14	7	15	16	14.5

9 Find the coordinates of the halfway point of the line segment joining point A to point B.

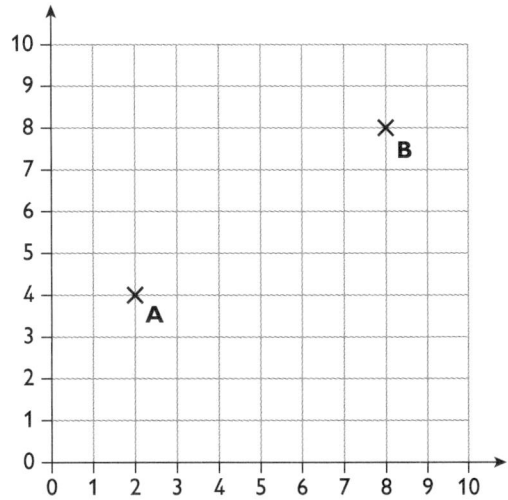

A	B	C	D	E
(4, 4)	(5, 6)	(6, 4)	(6, 5)	(5, 5)

10 Mae and Abdul share an amount of money in the ratio 3 : 2

Mae gets £10 more than Abdul.

How much money does Abdul get?

A	B	C	D	E
£10	£4	£20	£30	£50

Score: ………… / 10

Test 9

You have 10 minutes to complete this test.

You have 10 questions to complete within the given time.

Circle the letter above the correct answer.

(1) Work out 267 × 40

A	B	C	D	E
10 680	1068	16 080	82 680	10 480

(2) Six coffees cost £10.74

Work out the cost of 11 coffees.

A	B	C	D	E
£18.79	£19.69	£17.90	£18.59	£19.47

(3) What is 3 cubed?

A	B	C	D	E
3	6	9	27	333

(4) There are six episodes in a TV series.

Each episode lasts 45 minutes.

Work out the total time that the six episodes last.

A	B	C	D	E
3 hours	3.5 hours	4.5 hours	5 hours	5.5 hours

5. Susie does a survey to find out which pets people like best.

   She displays the information in the pictogram.

Dog	△ △ △
Cat	△ △ △
Fish	△
Hamster	△ △ △

   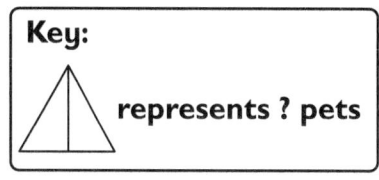

   Key:
   △ represents ? pets

   If Susie asked 54 people together, what does the question mark represent in the key?

A	B	C	D	E
2	3	4	5	6

6. In a competition, a player gets:

   3 points for each game they win

   1 point for a draw

   0 points for a loss.

   Ellen wins w games and draws d games.

   Which is the correct expression, in terms of w and d, for the total number of points Ellen gets?

A	B	C	D	E
$3w + 3d$	$w + 3d$	$3w + d$	$w + d$	$3w - d$

7. Look at the diagram.

   What is the size of angle x?

   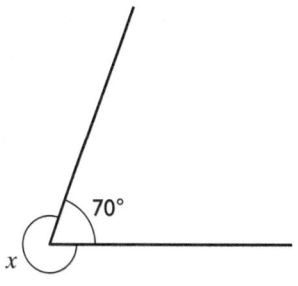

A	B	C	D	E
20°	110°	160°	300°	290°

Questions continue on next page

(8) Which calculation is correct?

A	B	C	D	E
30 ÷ (3 + 2) − 4 = 2	30 ÷ 3 + (2 − 4) = 2	(30 ÷ 3) + 2 − 4 = 2	30 ÷ (3 + 2 − 4) = 2	(30 ÷ 3 + 2) − 4 = 2

(9) Find the area of this shape.

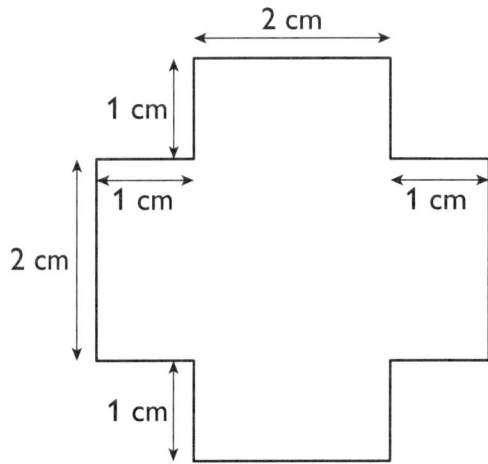

A	B	C	D	E
9 cm²	10 cm²	16 cm²	12 cm²	14 cm²

(10) A tour company is taking schoolchildren and teachers on a trip.

They can use coaches or minibuses:

Each coach can carry up to 54 passengers.

Each minibus can carry up to 14 passengers.

The schoolchildren and teachers going on the trip would fill exactly three coaches.

If the company uses only minibuses, how many would be needed?

A	B	C	D	E
10	11	12	13	14

Score: .... / 10

Test 10

You have 10 minutes to complete this test.

You have 10 questions to complete within the given time.

Circle the letter above the correct answer.

1) Which of these numbers has the smallest value?

A	B	C	D	E
0.2	0.04	1.01	1.76	0.91

2) This machine multiplies by 7 and then subtracts a number.

The input is 5 and the output is 27

5 → × 7 → − ▢ → 27

Which number should be in the grey box?

A	B	C	D	E
5	6	7	8	9

3) Which expression represents the perimeter of this shape?

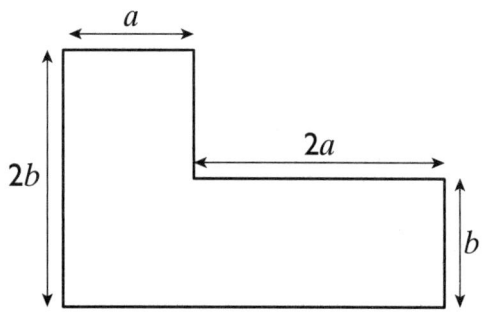

A	B	C	D	E
$3a + 2b$	$6a + 4b$	$a + 2b + 2a$	$6a + 2b$	$3a + 4b$

4) How many millimetres are there in 1 kilometre?

A	B	C	D	E
1 000 000	100 000	10 000	1000	100

Questions continue on next page

5) Today the temperature is 5°C.

Last night the temperature was −1°C.

What is the difference between these two temperatures?

A	B	C	D	E
6°C	5°C	−4°C	4°C	−6°C

6) The magic grid below contains number sequences that increase in equal steps horizontally and equal steps vertically.

26	33	X
39	46	53
Y	59	66

What are the two missing numbers, X and Y?

A	B	C	D	E
X = 38, Y = 50	X = 40, Y = 50	X = 39, Y = 52	X = 40, Y = 54	X = 40, Y = 52

7) How many lines of symmetry does this shape have?

A	B	C	D	E
1	2	3	4	5

8 There are 32 pupils in a class.

25% of the pupils bring a packed lunch every day.

The rest have a school lunch.

How many pupils have a school lunch?

A	B	C	D	E
8	24	12	20	28

9 How many vertices in total do these shapes have?

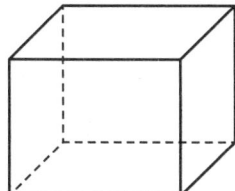
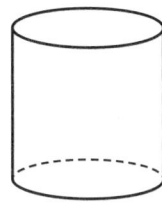

A	B	C	D	E
6	4	14	8	9

10 This graph can be used to change between inches and centimetres.

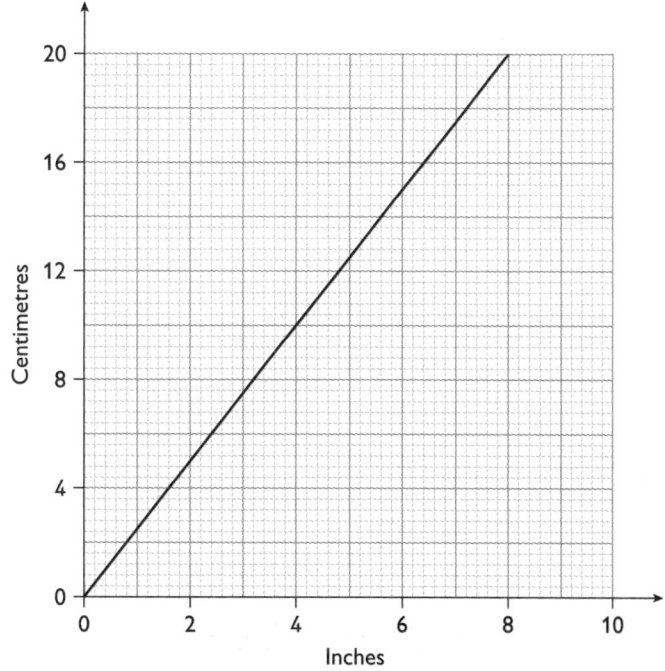

Use the graph to work out how many inches are in 200 centimetres.

A	B	C	D	E
8 inches	40 inches	80 inches	800 inches	20 inches

Score: ..../ 10

Test 11

You have 10 minutes to complete this test.

You have 10 questions to complete within the given time.

Circle the letter above the correct answer.

① What is this number written in digits?

Four hundred thousand, five hundred and seventy

A	B	C	D	E
400 507	405 070	400 570	40 050 070	40 050 700

② Which of these words does **not** have a horizontal line of symmetry?

CHEEK

BIKE

BOX

HIDE

HOAX

A	B	C	D	E
CHEEK	BIKE	BOX	HIDE	HOAX

③ Rohan weighs a bag of sand.

The scale shows its mass.

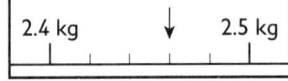

Rohan then adds another 500 grams of sand to the bag.

What is the new mass of the bag of sand?

A	B	C	D	E
2.96 kg	2.46 kg	2.93 kg	3.06 kg	3.6 kg

④ This shape is a trapezium. It can be split into three identical triangles in the way shown.

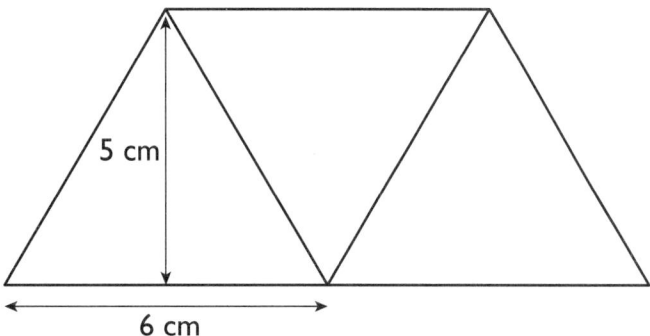

Work out the area of the trapezium.

A	B	C	D	E
90 cm²	45 cm²	30 cm²	15 cm²	60 cm²

⑤ The original price of a game is £36

In a sale, Vijay can get one-third off the original price.

Vijay buys the game in the sale using a £20 note and a £10 note.

How much change should he get?

A	B	C	D	E
£24	£0	£12	£6	£2

⑥ Erin makes this pie chart to show people's favourite holiday destinations.

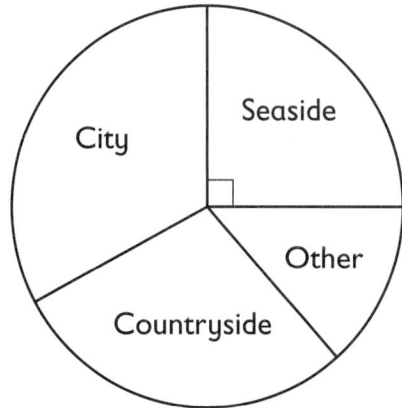

The pie chart represents 1700 people.

How many people chose the 'Seaside' as their favourite holiday destination?

A	B	C	D	E
400	425	1000	700	850

Questions continue on next page

7) Aygul wants to put up a fence around her garden.

Her garden measures 11 metres by 5 metres.

How many metres of fencing will Aygul need for the perimeter of her garden?

A	B	C	D	E
32 metres	16 metres	55 metres	21 metres	27 metres

8) The diagram shows an isosceles triangle.

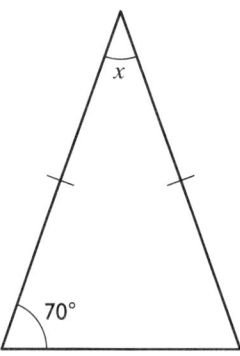

Work out the size of angle x.

A	B	C	D	E
70°	50°	90°	110°	40°

9) Which of these fractions is closest in value to 1?

$$\frac{1}{2} \quad \frac{2}{3} \quad \frac{5}{4} \quad \frac{7}{6} \quad \frac{7}{9}$$

A	B	C	D	E
$\frac{1}{2}$	$\frac{2}{3}$	$\frac{5}{4}$	$\frac{7}{6}$	$\frac{7}{9}$

10) Round this number to the nearest hundredth.

7.695

A	B	C	D	E
7.7	7.69	7.70	8.00	7.67

Score: .... / 10

Test 12

You have 10 minutes to complete this test.

You have 10 questions to complete within the given time.

Circle the letter above the correct answer.

1. Which factor of 60 is missing from this list?

    1, 2, 3, 4, 5, 6, 10, 12, 15, 30, 60

A	B	C	D	E
120	20	8	14	16

2. 16.8 × 525 = 8820

    What does 8.4 × 525 equal?

A	B	C	D	E
17 640	6640	2205	4410	4440

3. How many equilateral triangles will fit together to make a regular hexagon?

    Equilateral triangle **Regular hexagon**

    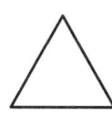 

A	B	C	D	E
4	5	6	7	8

Questions continue on next page

(4) P, Q and R are vertices of a parallelogram.

Point S is the fourth vertex of the parallelogram.

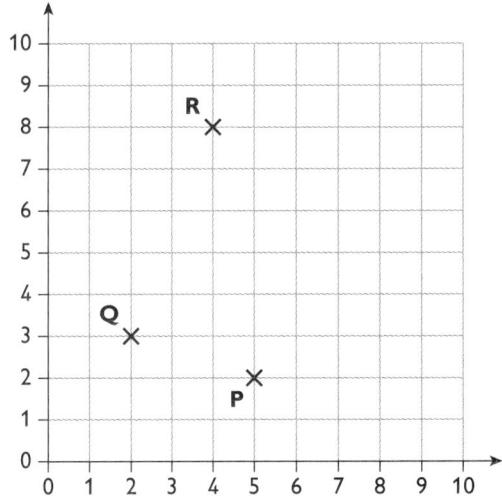

What are the coordinates of S?

A	B	C	D	E
(7, 7)	(6, 7)	(7, 6)	(6, 6)	(7, 8)

(5) Mary buys four apples and three bananas for £2.50

Two bananas cost 60p.

Work out the cost of five apples.

A	B	C	D	E
60p	£2	90p	£1.60	£1.50

(6) A sequence is generated using this rule:

Add the previous two numbers and subtract 1

The first six numbers in the sequence are:

5, 6, 10, 15, 24, 38

What is the eighth number in the sequence?

A	B	C	D	E
98	99	97	61	159

7. What is 25% of $\frac{3}{5}$ of 210?

A	B	C	D	E
52.5	10.5	157.5	31.5	87.5

8. This table shows the times taken by some people to run 5 km.

Time (minutes)	Number of people
0–20	3
21–25	16
26–30	27
31–35	13
36–40	3

Which one of these statements is true?

A	B	C	D	E
63 people ran the race altogether.	20 people had a time faster than 26 minutes.	Less than half of the people had a time slower than 25 minutes.	40 people had times between 21 and 35 minutes.	More than half of the people ran times faster than 31 minutes.

9. What is the obtuse angle between the clock hands?

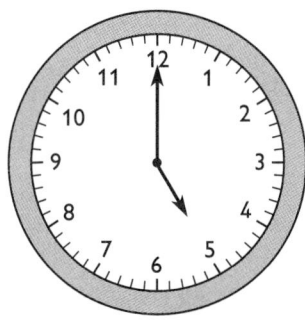

A	B	C	D	E
160°	15°	25°	120°	150°

10. What is 57.36 kilometres rounded to the nearest 100 metres?

A	B	C	D	E
5.7 km	6 km	57.3 km	57 km	57.4 km

Score: .... / 10

Test 13

You have 10 minutes to complete this test.

You have 10 questions to complete within the given time.

Circle the letter above the correct answer.

1. What is 152.97 rounded to the nearest tenth?

A	B	C	D	E
152.0	150.0	152.9	153.0	152.00

2. Which one of these calculations gives the smallest answer?

A	B	C	D	E
$\frac{3}{5}$ of 35	15% of 200	$\frac{2}{3}$ of 30	75% of 24	$\frac{1}{4}$ of 68

3. This diagram shows a cube that is made of wood.

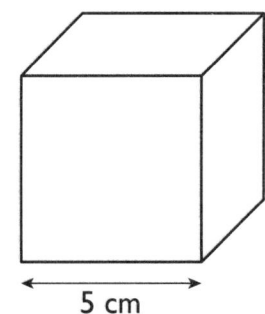

5 cm

What area of wood is needed to make all six faces?

A	B	C	D	E
150 cm²	25 cm²	100 cm²	125 cm²	75 cm²

4. A rope is 246 metres long.

The rope is cut into 15 pieces of equal length.

Each piece is a whole number of metres in length.

After the 15 pieces are cut, what length of rope is left over?

A	B	C	D	E
2 metres	4 metres	6 metres	8 metres	10 metres

5 A train leaves a station with **87** passengers.

At the next stop, **23** passengers get off.

If the remaining passengers are divided equally into **8** carriages, how many passengers are in each carriage?

A	B	C	D	E
12	10	8	6	4

6 Molly, Kim and Gigi share some money.

The money is divided into 10 equal parts.

Molly gets 3 parts, Kim gets 2 parts and Gigi gets 5 parts.

Gigi gets £10 more than Molly.

How much does Kim get?

A	B	C	D	E
£2	£3	£4	£5	£10

7 An isosceles triangle is placed on top of a square, as shown in the diagram.

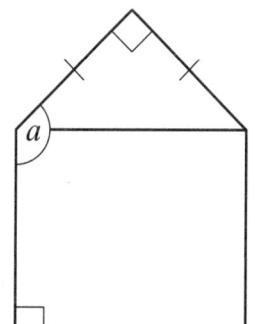

Work out the size of angle a.

A	B	C	D	E
90°	135°	45°	100°	140°

8 Lighthouse A and lighthouse B both flash at the same time.

They next flash at the same time 120 minutes later.

The amount of time between each flash of lighthouse A is different to the amount of time between each flash of lighthouse B.

What could be the amount of time between the flashes of each lighthouse?

A	B	C	D	E
Lighthouse A: 5 minutes Lighthouse B: 7 minutes	Lighthouse A: 9 minutes Lighthouse B: 10 minutes	Lighthouse A: 3 minutes Lighthouse B: 13 minutes	Lighthouse A: 8 minutes Lighthouse B: 15 minutes	Lighthouse A: 24 minutes Lighthouse B: 14 minutes

Questions continue on next page

9 Eve draws a rhombus.

Which property **must** her drawing have?

A	B	C	D	E
All angles are equal	At least one angle is a right angle	It has one line of symmetry	One diagonal is longer than the other	Opposite angles are equal

10 One day in July, Manchester had 7.36 hours of sunshine.

What is 7.36 hours in hours, minutes and seconds?

A	B	C	D	E
7 hours, 21 minutes, 36 seconds	7 hours, 36 minutes, 36 seconds	7 hours, 30 minutes, 36 seconds	7 hours, 21 minutes, 6 seconds	7 hours, 21 minutes, 30 seconds

Score: .... / 10

Test 14

You have 10 minutes to complete this test.

You have 10 questions to complete within the given time.

Circle the letter above the correct answer.

1) Work out 12 + 14 × 5

A	B	C	D	E
82	52	130	102	80

2) Kaylia measures the lengths of five worms.

They are 5 cm, 7.2 cm, 3.7 cm, 1.9 cm and 4.6 cm.

What is the total length of the worms?

A	B	C	D	E
17.9 cm	18.1 cm	24.2 cm	22.4 cm	19.3 cm

3) What is the answer to this calculation?

5 730 000 + 573 000 + 5730 = ?

A	B	C	D	E
6 308 730	1 151 730	11 465 730	6 360 300	638 730

4) The bar chart shows the number of points scored by Shaun and Amina in a game from Monday to Friday one week.

Which of these statements is **not** true?

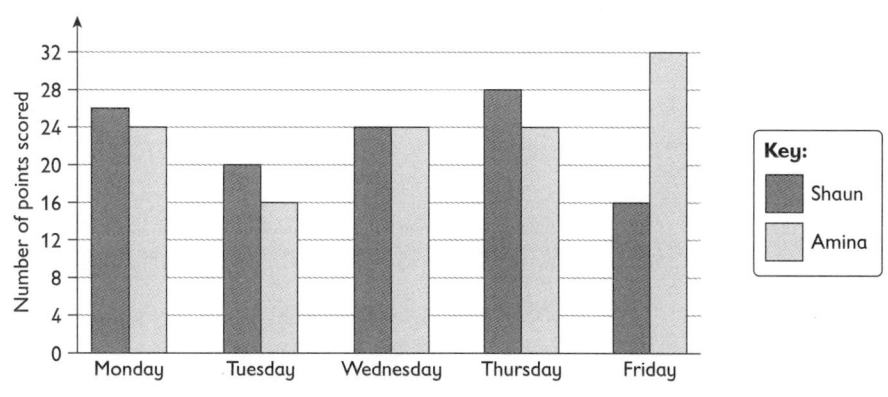

A	B	C	D	E
Overall, Amina scored more points than Shaun.	Overall, Shaun scored 8 points fewer than Amina.	Amina scored the highest number of points in a single day.	Shaun and Amina scored 16 points on different days.	The biggest difference between their points was on Friday.

Questions continue on next page

5 Kylie timed herself running 400 metres over four weeks.

Her times were:

2 minutes 9 seconds

1 minute 58 seconds

1 minute 49 seconds

1 minute 44 seconds

What is the difference between her fastest and slowest times, and what is the difference between her middle two times?

A	B	C	D	E
15 seconds; 9 seconds	25 seconds; 9 seconds	15 seconds; 11 seconds	25 seconds; 11 seconds	35 seconds; 9 seconds

6 There are adults and children in a cinema.

There are 144 children.

25% of the people at the cinema are adults.

Work out the total number of people in the cinema.

A	B	C	D	E
169	576	192	48	288

7 The diagram shows nine identical squares inside a rectangle.

The length of the rectangle is 12 cm.

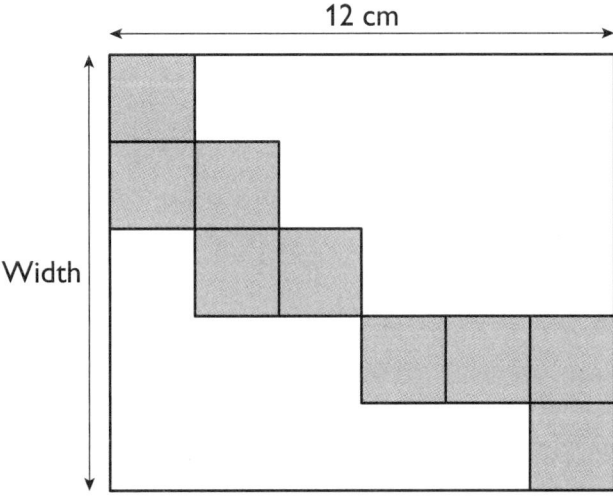

What is the width of the rectangle?

A	B	C	D	E
12 cm	6 cm	5 cm	8 cm	10 cm

(8) Here is part of a bus timetable:

Appletown	0804
Banbridge	0809
Castleford	0838
Debden	0901
Engleby	0939

How long does the journey take from Banbridge to Debden?

A	B	C	D	E
1 hour 8 minutes	1 hour 2 minutes	59 minutes	51 minutes	52 minutes

(9) Three apples and two oranges cost £2.55

One apple costs £0.55

How much does one orange cost?

A	B	C	D	E
£0.90	£4.50	£0.55	£0.45	£0.65

(10) Katya measured the length of her garden.

It was 15.0 metres to the nearest tenth of a metre.

Which of the following could have been the actual length of her garden?

A	B	C	D	E
14.95 m	15.05 m	14.09 m	14.05 m	15.09 m

Score: .... / 10

Test 15

You have 10 minutes to complete this test.

You have 10 questions to complete within the given time.

Circle the letter above the correct answer.

① At an airport, 12 flights departed on Monday and 16 flights departed on Tuesday.

Each flight had 124 passengers on board.

How many passengers in total departed on these two days?

A	B	C	D	E
3742	3472	3372	2472	1240

② A regular polygon has an interior angle of 108°

What is the name of this polygon?

A	B	C	D	E
Equilateral triangle	Pentagon	Hexagon	Heptagon	Octagon

③ The diameter of a 5p coin is 18 mm.

Sally has £2.40 worth of 5p coins and creates a line with her coins.

Each coin in the line touches the next coin in the line, as shown.

How long is Sally's line of coins?

A	B	C	D	E
8.64 cm	82.8 cm	79.2 cm	864 cm	86.4 cm

(4) Dan is making a picture frame.

He has 1.2 metres of wood for the frame.

Each side of the frame is a whole number in centimetres.

What is the largest area that the picture frame can create?

A	B	C	D	E
1000 cm²	800 cm²	900 cm²	1200 cm²	600 cm²

(5) Which calculation gives the smallest answer?

A	B	C	D	E
6 + 7 × 8 − 5	5 + 8 × 7 − 6	7 + 5 × 6 − 8	8 + 7 × 6 − 5	8 + 7 × 5 − 6

(6) What is the difference between the square of 25 and the square of 15?

A	B	C	D	E
10	100	625	225	400

(7) A jumper costs £80 but is on sale for 25% off.

A scarf costs £50 before a 10% discount.

How much cheaper is the scarf than the jumper after the reductions?

A	B	C	D	E
£15	£5	£10	£30	£20

Questions continue on next page

(8) A loaf of bread is cut into 20 slices.

Ben eats $\frac{3}{5}$ of the slices, and Fatima eats $\frac{1}{4}$ of the slices.

How many slices are left?

A	B	C	D	E
6	5	4	3	2

(9) The number 17 bus leaves a bus station at 9.45 am and takes 1 hour and 50 minutes to reach its destination.

The number 18 bus leaves the same bus station at 10.30 am and takes 1 hour and 10 minutes to reach the same destination.

Which bus arrives first, and by how many minutes?

A	B	C	D	E
Number 17 by 5 minutes	Number 18 by 5 minutes	Number 17 by 15 minutes	Number 18 by 15 minutes	Number 17 by 10 minutes

(10) The coordinate grid shows three vertices of a parallelogram.

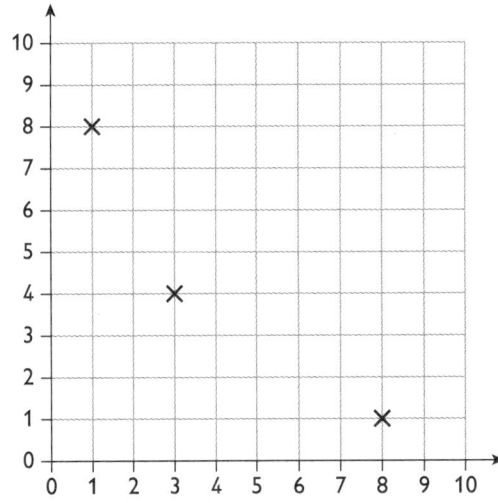

What are the coordinates of the fourth vertex of the parallelogram?

A	B	C	D	E
(6, 6)	(5, 6)	(8, 8)	(6, 5)	(4, 6)

Score: .... / 10

Test 16

You have 10 minutes to complete this test.

You have 10 questions to complete within the given time.

Circle the letter above the correct answer.

1) A shop sells 12 oranges for £4.20

   How much would 15 oranges cost?

A	B	C	D	E
£5.20	£5.50	£6.25	£5.25	£6.20

2) A rectangle has a perimeter of 48 cm.

   One of the longer sides is 16 cm.

   What is the length of one of the shorter sides?

A	B	C	D	E
8 cm	4 cm	6 cm	12 cm	16 cm

3) Pat is three times as old as his sister now.

   In five years, Pat will be twice as old as his sister.

   How old is Pat now?

A	B	C	D	E
7	10	12	15	5

4) How many cubic centimetres are in a cubic metre?

A	B	C	D	E
100	1000	10 000	100 000	1 000 000

Questions continue on next page

(5) The pictogram shows the number of people who visited a leisure centre one day and the activities they chose.

Activity	Number of people
Swim	3 octagons
Gym	3 octagons + 1 quarter
Sauna	1 octagon + 1 portion

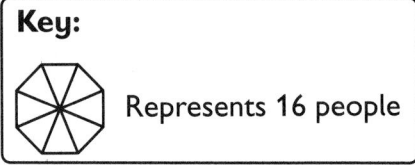

Key: Represents 16 people

How many people chose the gym?

A	B	C	D	E
48	51	54	56	64

(6) Five packs of tea bags are available in a supermarket.

Pack A	Pack B	Pack C	Pack D	Pack E
240 tea bags for £4.80	120 tea bags for £3.60	100 tea bags for £1.75	50 tea bags for £1.60	160 tea bags for £3.20

Which pack offers the best value for money?

A	B	C	D	E
Pack A	Pack B	Pack C	Pack D	Pack E

(7) Here is a number machine:

Input → × 4 → − 7 → Output

What is the input when the output is 25?

A	B	C	D	E
8	93	4.5	72	16

(8) Here is a number sequence:

Find the two missing numbers to complete the sequence.

A	B	C	D	E
−26 and −12	−27 and −14	−26 and −13	−26 and −14	−27 and −13

(9) The container is full of water.

The water is going to be used to fill cups that can hold 175 ml of water.

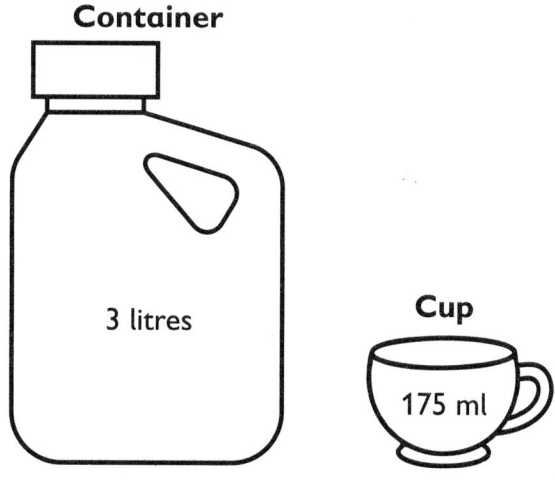

How many cups can be completely filled with water from the container?

A	B	C	D	E
14	15	16	17	18

(10) Work out   0.5 × 0.6

A	B	C	D	E
30	0.3	3	0.03	0.003

Score: .... / 10

Test 17

You have **10 minutes** to complete this test.

You have **10 questions** to complete within the given time.

Circle the letter above the correct answer.

1) Which of these statements is most likely to be true?

A	B	C	D	E
My two-storey house is 0.2 kilometres tall.	My two-storey house is 9 metres tall.	My two-storey house is 200 centimetres tall.	My two-storey house is 1000 millimetres tall.	My two-storey house is 27 metres tall.

2) What is 199.99 rounded to 1 decimal place?

A	B	C	D	E
199.9	199.0	199.10	200.0	200.1

3) The pointer turns anticlockwise from north to south-west.

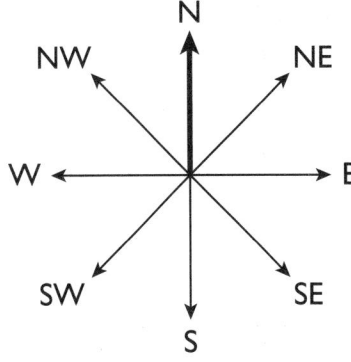

What angle does it turn through?

A	B	C	D	E
135°	125°	225°	165°	120°

52

④ A tank holds 120 litres of water.

It leaks at a rate of 4 litres every 15 minutes.

How many hours will it take for the tank to empty completely?

A	B	C	D	E
6.5 hours	7 hours	7.5 hours	7.30 hours	8 hours

⑤ What is the sum of all prime numbers between 20 and 30?

A	B	C	D	E
29	73	79	100	52

⑥ What is the difference between 75% of 152 and 60% of 240?

A	B	C	D	E
30	88	114	44	106

⑦ Which pair of lines are perpendicular?

A	B	C	D	E

⑧ The temperature in Alaska on one night in December was −9°C.

The temperature in Toronto on the same night was −1°C.

How much warmer was it in Toronto than in Alaska?

A	B	C	D	E
−8°C	10°C	−10°C	8°C	9°C

Questions continue on next page

(9) The pie chart shows information about the languages studied by a group of students.

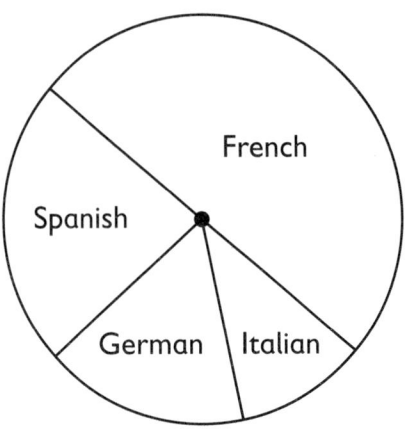

48 students study French.

How many students are there in the group altogether?

A	B	C	D	E
48	96	100	140	240

(10) In a school classroom, one row of desks is set up with 50 cm between them, as shown.

Each desk is 1 metre wide, and each end desk is put against the wall.

How many desks are in one row of a classroom that is 16 metres wide?

A	B	C	D	E
16	12	10	9	11

Score: ………… / 10

Test 18

You have 10 minutes to complete this test.

You have 10 questions to complete within the given time.

Circle the letter above the correct answer.

1) What is the value of the digit 6 in this number?

    97.0761

A	B	C	D	E
6 ones	6 tenths	6 hundredths	6 thousandths	6 ten thousandths

2) Ali has six identical equilateral triangles.

    He fits them all together to make a regular polygon.

    Which regular polygon does he make?

A	B	C	D	E
Square	Pentagon	Hexagon	Heptagon	Octagon

3) This graph converts inches to centimetres.

    Use the graph to change 16 inches to centimetres.

A	B	C	D	E
20 cm	40 cm	36 cm	48 cm	32 cm

Questions continue on next page

(4) Will visits a café.

He chooses one starter and one main from the menu below.

Menu	
Starter	**Main**
Soup	Pasta
Garlic bread	Pizza
Melon	Salad

How many different combinations can Will choose?

A	B	C	D	E
5	6	7	8	9

(5) Joe and Jill saved a total of £482

Jill saved £34 more than Joe.

How much did Joe save?

A	B	C	D	E
£241	£207	£224	£275	£334

(6) Fifty Year 6 pupils were asked whether they had a brother or a sister, or both.

　　30 had a brother.

　　25 had a sister.

　　6 had neither a brother nor a sister.

Some of this information is shown in the diagram.

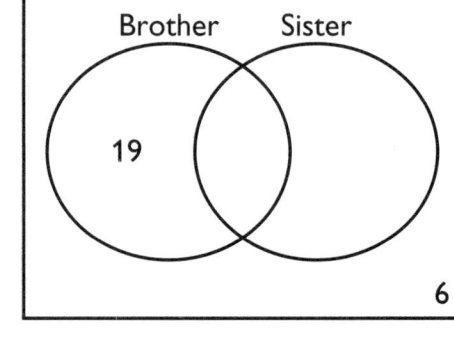

How many pupils only had a sister?

A	B	C	D	E
25	6	11	14	19

(7) A baker uses 2.5 kg of flour for cakes, 1.75 kg of flour for bread and 800 g of flour for pastries.

How much flour does the baker use in total?

A	B	C	D	E
5.5 kg	5.05 kg	4.33 kg	12.25 kg	4.05 kg

(8) The table below shows some information about how 100 pupils travel to school.

	Walk	Cycle	Car or bus	Total
Girls	15			52
Boys		22	8	
Total			19	100

Work out the total number of pupils who walk to school.

A	B	C	D	E
33	18	52	81	48

(9) This shape is made using equilateral triangles of side length 5 cm.

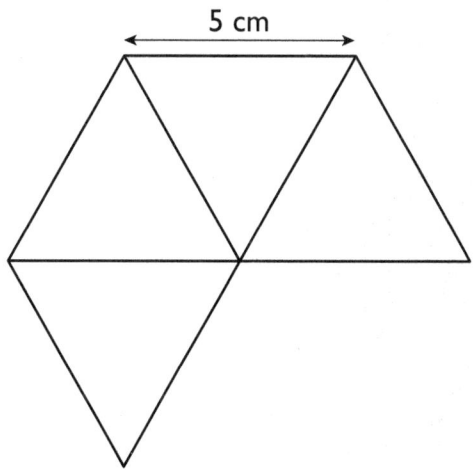

Work out the perimeter of the shape.

A	B	C	D	E
50 cm	45 cm	40 cm	30 cm	25 cm

(10) The price of a pair of trainers is reduced in a sale by 25%.

If the sale price of the trainers is £60, what was the original price?

A	B	C	D	E
£75	£90	£100	£80	£85

Score: .... / 10

Test 19

You have 10 minutes to complete this test.

You have 10 questions to complete within the given time.

Circle the letter above the correct answer.

(1) Work out the difference between 3 hours 25 minutes and $1\frac{1}{4}$ hours.

A	B	C	D	E
1 hour 10 minutes	1 hour 25 minutes	1 hour 50 minutes	2 hours 10 minutes	2 hours 20 minutes

(2) A robot is guided along the grey squares through this maze.

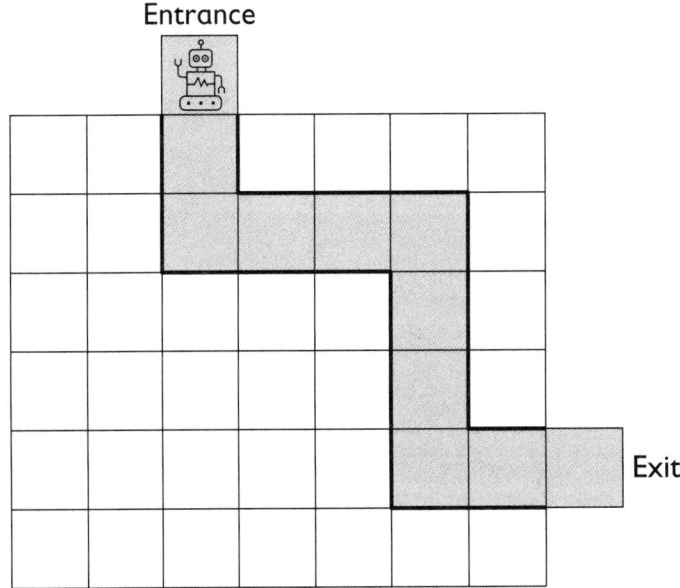

The robot starts on the square marked 'Entrance' and finishes on the square marked 'Exit'.

The robot can only move FORWARD, TURN RIGHT 90° and TURN LEFT 90°.

Which instructions will guide the robot through the maze?

A	B	C	D	E
FORWARD 1, TURN LEFT 90°, FORWARD 2, TURN RIGHT 90°, FORWARD 2, TURN LEFT 90°, FORWARD 1	FORWARD 2, TURN LEFT 90°, FORWARD 3, TURN RIGHT 90°, FORWARD 3, TURN RIGHT 90°, FORWARD 2	FORWARD 2, TURN LEFT 90°, FORWARD 3, TURN RIGHT 90°, FORWARD 3, TURN LEFT 90°, FORWARD 2	FORWARD 2, TURN RIGHT 90°, FORWARD 2, TURN RIGHT 90°, FORWARD 3, TURN LEFT 90°, FORWARD 2	FORWARD 2, TURN RIGHT 90°, FORWARD 3, TURN LEFT 90°, FORWARD 3, TURN RIGHT 90°, FORWARD 2

(3) The six-sided shape shown below is made from two identical rectangles.

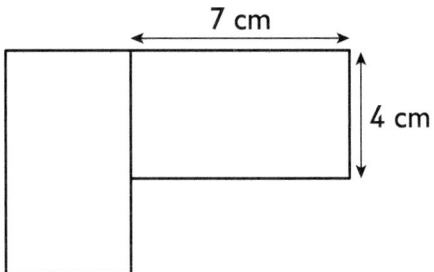

Work out the perimeter of the six-sided shape.

A	B	C	D	E
37 cm	36 cm	44 cm	40 cm	42 cm

(4) Three pens cost £3.54

Work out the cost of seven pens.

A	B	C	D	E
£8.26	£7.56	£7.08	£8.12	£8.16

(5) Bulbs are planted in a field in rows.

Each row has 8 bulbs.

How many rows will there be if 1360 bulbs are planted?

A	B	C	D	E
10 880	170	160	340	230

(6) The diagram shows a square and an equilateral triangle.

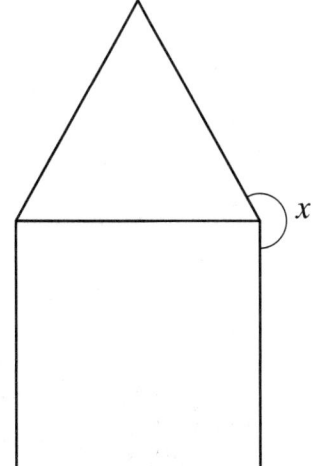

Work out the size of angle x.

A	B	C	D	E
30°	110°	210°	300°	270°

Questions continue on next page

(7) Which of the following has three numbers that are all prime numbers?

A	B	C	D	E
1, 2, 11	1, 13, 25	2, 5, 39	3, 5, 15	2, 23, 37

(8) The diagram shows a sequence of patterns made using counters.

Pattern 1   **Pattern 2**   **Pattern 3**

How many counters in total would be needed to make pattern number 4?

A	B	C	D	E
17	20	16	18	21

(9) A plan of a garden is drawn using a scale of 3 cm to 10 m.

On the plan, the garden is 7.5 cm long.

What is the real length of the garden?

A	B	C	D	E
7.5 m	10 m	20 m	25 m	30 m

(10) Here are five triangles:

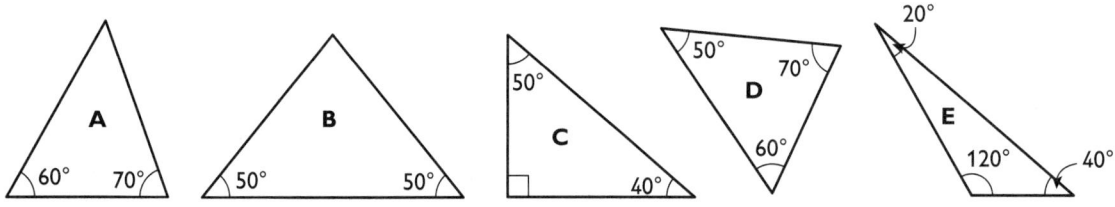

Which triangle is isosceles?

A	B	C	D	E
Triangle A	Triangle B	Triangle C	Triangle D	Triangle E

Score: .... / 10

Test 20

You have 10 minutes to complete this test.

You have 10 questions to complete within the given time.

Circle the letter above the correct answer.

1) A number is squared and then squared again.

   The answer is 81.

   What is the number?

A	B	C	D	E
8	3	7	9	11

2) Which number goes into the box to make this calculation correct?

   $2\frac{2}{3} + \square = 6$

A	B	C	D	E
$4\frac{1}{3}$	$3\frac{1}{3}$	$2\frac{1}{3}$	$3\frac{2}{3}$	$2\frac{2}{3}$

3) An equilateral triangle is reflected in the mirror line.

   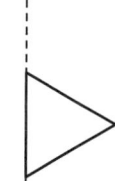

   The shape that is made is a quadrilateral.

   What type of quadrilateral is it?

A	B	C	D	E
Rhombus	Square	Trapezium	Kite	Rectangle

4) Maya plants 280 seeds.

   $\frac{5}{7}$ of the seeds grow into flowers.

   How many seeds do **not** grow into flowers?

A	B	C	D	E
40	200	80	56	224

Questions continue on next page

5) A recipe for 12 mince pies requires 300 g of plain flour.

Susie has 475 g of plain flour and plenty of all the other ingredients.

How many mince pies can Susie make?

A	B	C	D	E
20	19	18	17	16

6) Ria has a 3D shape.

The shape has eight vertices.

Which of these could be Ria's shape?

A	B	C	D	E
Cylinder	Square-based pyramid	Triangular prism	Octahedron	Cube

7) Maria wants to buy as many pencils as she can.

She has £5 to spend.

Each pencil costs £0.35

How much change should Maria get from £5?

A	B	C	D	E
£0.15	£0.25	£0.30	£0.20	£0.10

8) Nick buys headphones for £20

The headphones have been reduced by 20% in a sale.

What was the original price of the headphones?

A	B	C	D	E
£22	£25	£24	£30	£28

(9) The bar chart shows the number of goals scored by a hockey team in games this season.

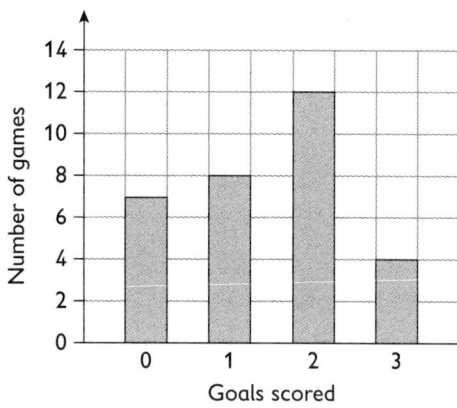

What is the total number of goals scored by the team?

A	B	C	D	E
31	29	16	44	24

(10) The large hexagon is formed from 24 identical equilateral triangles.

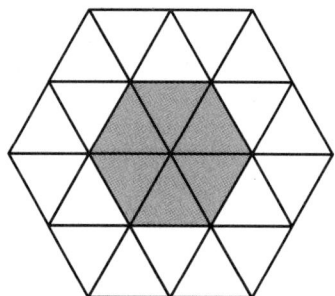

The perimeter of the large hexagon is 36 cm.

What is the perimeter of the inner, shaded hexagon?

A	B	C	D	E
18 cm	16 cm	24 cm	12 cm	30 cm

Score: ………… / 10

Test 21

You have 10 minutes to complete this test.

You have 10 questions to complete within the given time.

Circle the letter above the correct answer.

1 Work out the value of $(0.12)^2$

A	B	C	D	E
0.144	1.44	14.4	0.0144	0.00144

2 A container contains 3.6 litres of water when it is half full.

How much **more** water is required to make the container two-thirds full?

A	B	C	D	E
4.8 litres	1.2 litres	7.2 litres	2.4 litres	5.4 litres

3 In this pentagon, the three angles marked y are the same size.

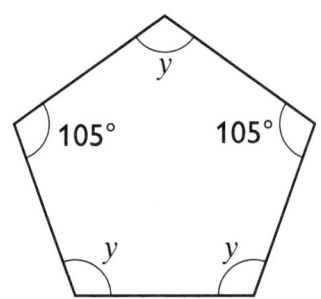

What is the size of each angle marked y?

A	B	C	D	E
105°	50°	170°	100°	110°

4 A number rounded to the nearest 10 is 1000

The range of possible values of the number is between _____ and _____.

Which pair of numbers fills the blank spaces correctly?

A	B	C	D	E
990 and 1010	995 and 1050	995 and 1005	990 and 1005	950 and 1050

⑤ Abi makes an open box from this flat piece of card.

She cuts out four identical squares from the corners, as shown, and then folds up the card.

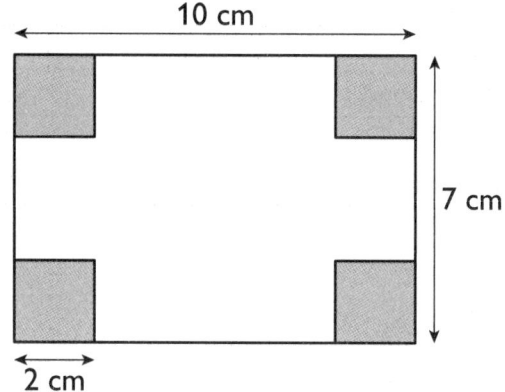

What is the capacity of the box Abi makes?

A	B	C	D	E
36 cm³	70 cm³	80 cm³	84 cm³	18 cm³

⑥ Which answer shows the correct numbers of faces, edges and vertices of a triangular prism?

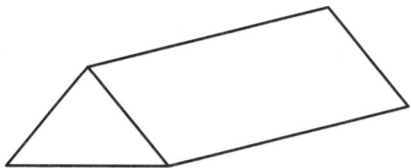

A	B	C	D	E
6 faces 9 edges 5 vertices	9 faces 5 edges 6 vertices	5 faces 6 edges 9 vertices	6 faces 5 edges 9 vertices	5 faces 9 edges 6 vertices

⑦ Use the multiplication 24 × 36 = 864

to work out 2.4 × 36 000

A	B	C	D	E
864	8640	86 400	864 000	86.4

Questions continue on next page

(8) Here is part of a bus timetable:

Clapham Junction	10 13	10 30	10 33
Eccles Road	10 26	↓	10 41
Sisters Avenue	10 29	10 39	10 45
Forthbridge Road	10 32	↓	10 48
Cedars Road	10 40	↓	10 55
Clapham Common	10 47	10 49	11 00

Seb is at Sisters Avenue.

He needs to be at Cedars Road by 11:00

What time is the latest bus he can catch from Sisters Avenue?

A	B	C	D	E
10:29	10:39	10:55	10:45	10:40

(9) Change 4000 millimetres into kilometres.

A	B	C	D	E
4 km	0.4 km	0.04 km	0.004 km	0.0004 km

(10) What percentage of the rectangle below is shaded?

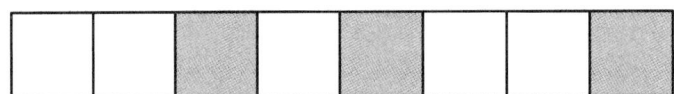

A	B	C	D	E
38%	30%	35%	32%	37.5%

Test 22

You have 10 minutes to complete this test.

You have 10 questions to complete within the given time.

Circle the letter above the correct answer.

1) Which number is halfway between 3.4 and 4.1?

A	B	C	D	E
3.7	3.75	3.65	3.8	3.85

2) What is −2 multiplied by itself and then multiplied by itself again?

A	B	C	D	E
6	−6	8	−8	4

3) When Bob was 31, Tilly was 8.

Now Bob is twice as old as Tilly.

How old is Tilly now?

A	B	C	D	E
46	17	22	20	23

4) What is the percentage increase from £56 to £63?

A	B	C	D	E
12.5%	10%	12%	13%	7%

Questions continue on next page

5) The triangle below is reflected in the dashed line.

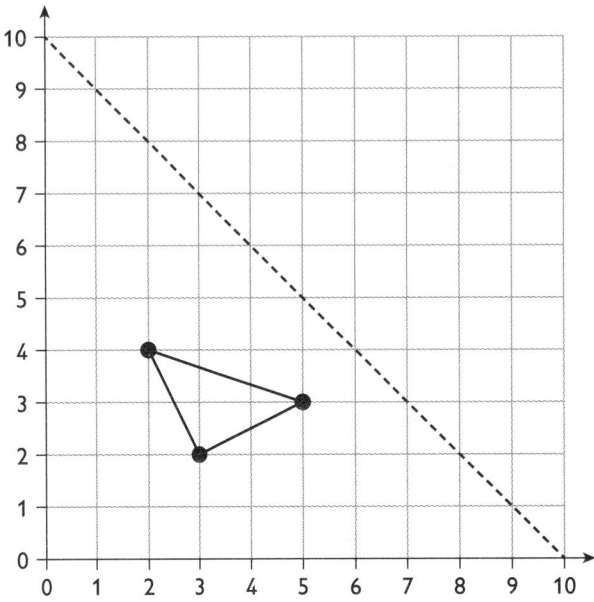

What are the coordinates of the reflected triangle?

A	B	C	D	E
(6, 8) (8, 7) (7, 5)	(5, 7) (7, 8) (8, 6)	(6, 8) (7, 8) (7, 5)	(8, 6) (7, 8) (7, 5)	(6, 8) (8, 7) (7, 6)

6) A comic costs £3.40 and a newspaper costs £1.60

Noah spends exactly £23 on comics and newspapers.

How many newspapers does he buy?

A	B	C	D	E
3	7	5	8	10

7) What are the missing two numbers in this sequence?

☐, 2.5, 1.25, 0.625, ☐

A	B	C	D	E
4 and 0.3	5 and 0.3125	5 and 0	3.75 and 0	3.75 and −0.625

8) The diagram shows a scale drawing of a woman of average height standing next to a tree.

Work out an estimate for the real height of the tree in metres.

A	B	C	D	E
9.5 m	8 m	6.4 m	4 m	2 m

9) In the addition shown, the different shapes represent different single digits.

Which digit does the triangle represent?

A	B	C	D	E
4	5	6	7	8

10) A square piece of paper is folded exactly in half and then in half again.

Which of the following shapes could **not** be the final shape?

A	B	C	D	E

Score: .... / 10

Answers

Key abbreviations: °C: degrees centigrade, cm: centimetre, g: gram, kg: kilogram, km: kilometre, m: metre, ml: millilitre, mm: millimetre

Test 1

Q1 D

Q2 D
A rectangle has two pairs of equal sides and so the dimensions must sum to 10 cm.
4 + 5 = 9 and so cannot be correct.

Q3 C
ml is the best measure for the amount of water in a glass.

Q4 B
From the graph, 45 litres = 10 gallons so 90 litres (45 × 2) will be (10 × 2) 20 gallons.

Q5 A
£2.40 + £3.25 + £3.25 + £2.95 = £11.85
£20 − £11.85 = £8.15 change

Q6 C
−9 − 17 = −26

Q7 A
$\frac{1}{3}$ of 300 = 100
300 − 100 = 200 left
$\frac{2}{5}$ of 200 = 80
200 − 80 = 120 sweets left

Q8 E
There are 180° on a straight line.
180° − 135° = 45°

Q9 B
6^2 = 36
8^2 = 64
36 + 64 = 100

Q10 A
The shape has eight sides so it is an octagon.

Test 2

Q1 B
167 ÷ 13 = 12 remainder 11

Q2 C

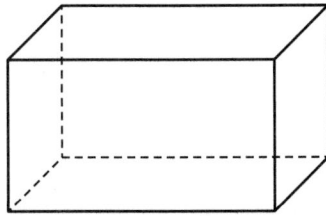

A cuboid has six faces.

Q3 B
$\frac{1}{3}$ of £48 = £48 ÷ 3 = £16 off
£48 − £16 = £32

Q4 A
The sequence increases by 4 each time.
−3, 1, 5, 9, 13, 17, 21, 25, 29, 33

Q5 D
There are 3 white triangles out of a total of 14 cards, so the probability is $\frac{3}{14}$

Q6 E
Converting all the measurements into metres:
400 cm = 4 m
0.003 km = 3 m
2500 mm = 2.5 m
2 m = 2 m
In order of size (smallest first):
2 m, 2500 mm, 0.003 km and 400 cm

Q7 D
5 × 85p = 425p = £4.25
£7.85 − £4.25 = £3.60
£3.60 ÷ 9 = £0.40 = 40p for each ruler

Q8 C
90° on the pie chart is $\frac{1}{4}$ of the balloons so there are
48 ÷ 4 = 12 blue balloons
48 − 12 = 36
36 balloons are not blue.

Q9 A
39 + 9 + 24 + 17 = 89

Q10 E
10% of £80 = £8
20% of £80 = £16
£80 − £16 = £64

Test 3

Q1 C
302 706

Q2 A
−5 + 7 × 2 = −5 + 14 = 9

Q3 C
8

Q4 E
7631 − 1367 = 6264

Q5 B
320 cm + 90 cm = 410 cm = 4.1 m

Q6 D
Each whole symbol represents 6 traffic cones.

Q7 A
Shape A has five sides (not four) so is not a quadrilateral.

Q8 E
$\frac{4}{6}$ can be simplified to $\frac{2}{3}$

Q9 D
Let the number be N. $(N ÷ 2 − 6)^2 = 16$
Square root both sides to get $N ÷ 2 − 6 = 4$
Add 6 to both sides. $N ÷ 2 = 10$
Multiply both sides by 2. $N = 20$

Q10 D
$2a − 7 = 21$
Add 7 to both sides. $2a = 28$
Divide by 2. $a = 14$

Test 4

Q1 C
$52 \div 13 = 4$
$4 \times 5 = 20$

Q2 D
$4 \text{ cm} \times 4 \text{ cm} \times 6 = 96 \text{ cm}^2$

Q3 B
$300\,000 - 6700 = 293\,300$

Q4 D
$172 \div 21.5 = 8$ weeks

Q5 A
11.45 am + 15 minutes = 12 noon
12 noon + 32 minutes = 12.32 pm
15 + 32 = 47 minutes

Q6 E
30p = 10% of £3
So 60p = 20%

Q7 B
36

Q8 D
$9^2 = 81$
$\sqrt{49} = 7$
$81 - 7 = 74$

Q9 E
£2.10 + £0.75 + £1.79 + £1.12 = £5.76
£10 − £5.76 = £4.24

Q10 A
$\frac{3}{4} = \frac{9}{12}$ (greatest)
$\frac{5}{12}$ (smallest)
$\frac{9}{12} - \frac{5}{12} = \frac{4}{12} = \frac{1}{3}$

Test 5

Q1 B
13 + 3 = 16 blue counters
10 : 16 = 5 : 8

Q2 C
$\frac{1}{4}$ of 24 = 6
$\frac{2}{3}$ of 6 = 4

Q3 B
3 + 4 = 7
$\frac{12}{12} - \frac{7}{12} = \frac{5}{12}$

Q4 E
$3 \times 4 = 12$ cups of flour
$2 \times 4 = 8$ cups of sugar

Q5 C
$7 \text{ cm} \times 4 = 28 \text{ cm}$

Q6 B
14:45 + 15 minutes is 15:00
15:00 + 1 hour = 16:00
16:00 + 20 minutes = 16:20
15 minutes + 1 hour + 20 minutes = 1 hour 35 minutes

Q7 A
£1.25 + £2.75 = £4.00
£5.50 − £4.00 = £1.50

Q8 D
12 + 5 = 17
17 − 5 = 12
$x = 17$

Q9 A
$56 + 63 + 71 + 78 + 82 = 350$
$350 \div 5 = 70$

Q10 E
January = 46 books, February = 50 books, March = 55 books, April = 52 books, May = 54 books
55 − 46 = 9

Test 6

Q1 C
The arrow labelled C is pointing to 2.44

Q2 D
$180° - 129° = 51°$

Q3 B

Q4 A
7   4   1   −2   −5   −8   −11
−14   −17   **−20**

Q5 E
35 stars were earned after 3 weeks and 54 stars after 4 weeks, so 19 stars were earned during the fourth week.

Q6 B
160 is a multiple of 80, not a factor of 80.

Q7 A
10% of £12.80 = £1.28
£12.80 − £1.28 = £11.52

Q8 E
48 cm = 480 mm
$480 \div 0.6 = 4800 \div 6 = 800$

Q9 C
There is only one G section so two Gs is the least likely outcome.

Q10 B
$5 \times 1.6 = 10 \times 0.8 = 8$

Test 7

Q1 C
$-4°C + 9°C = 5°C$

Q2 D
3.4 kg = 3400 g
3400 g − 500 g = 2900 g = 2.9 kg

Q3 B
$2 \times 45 = 90$
240 cm − 90 cm = 150 cm left
$150 \div 40 = 3$ remainder 30 cm
Petra can cut three pieces 40 cm long.

Q4 C
$(-3)^2 = -3 \times -3 = 9$

Q5 C
$2(1 + 3) + 2(2 + 1) = 14$ cm

Q6 A
$\frac{2}{3} = \frac{12}{18}$

Q7 E
12 + 9 + 6 + 13 = 40

Q8 E
Range is largest − smallest
9.01 − 0.23 = 8.78

Q9 B
7 + 14 = 21
21 ÷ 2 = 10.5

Q10	D
	38 ≈ 40
	307 ≈ 300
	40 × 300 = 12 000

Test 8

Q1	B
Q2	B
	12 × 27 = 270 + 54 = 324
Q3	A
	The sequence adds 10 each time.
	−21 + 10 = **−11**
	−11 + 10 = −1
	−1 + 10 = **9**
	9 + 10 = 19
Q4	D
	8 friends as 153 ÷ 17 = 9 (and Harry counts as one)
Q5	E
	15% of £120 = £12 + £6 = £18
Q6	D
Q7	D
	£1.35 × 4 = £5.40 (cost of cakes)
	£10 − £5.40 − £2.20 = £2.40 (cost of drinks)
	£2.40 ÷ 4 = £0.60 or 60p
Q8	A
	2 × **14** + 7 = 35
Q9	B
	From A to B is 6 units along and 4 units up.
	The halfway point will be 3 units along and 2 units up from A, which is (5, 6).
Q10	C
	One part is £10 (3 − 2 = 1)
	Abdul gets 2 parts so 2 × £10 = £20

Test 9

Q1	A
	267 × 4 = 534 + 534 = 1068
	1068 × 10 = 10 680
Q2	B
	£10.74 ÷ 6 = £1.79 (cost of one coffee)
	£1.79 × 11 = £19.69
Q3	D
	3 cubed = 3 × 3 × 3 = 27
Q4	C
	45 × 6 = 270
	4 hours = 60 × 4 = 240 minutes
	270 − 240 = 30 minutes left over
	4 hours and 30 minutes = 4.5 hours
Q5	E
	There are 8 full shapes plus 2 half shapes in the pictogram, making 9 full shapes in total.
	54 ÷ 9 = 6
Q6	C
Q7	E
	360° − 70° = 290°
Q8	A
	30 ÷ (3 + 2) − 4 = 2
	30 ÷ 5 = 6
	6 − 4 = 2

Q9	D
	The shape is a square 4 cm by 4 cm with 1 cm² squares cut from each corner.
	The area is (4 cm × 4 cm) − (4 cm × 1 cm) =
	16 cm² − 4 cm² = 12 cm²
Q10	C
	54 × 3 = 162
	162 ÷ 14 = 11 remainder 8, so 12 minibuses are needed.

Test 10

Q1	B
Q2	D
	5 × 7 − **8** = 27
Q3	B
	The shape has sides of $a, b, 2a, b, 3a$ and $2b$.
	$a, b, 2a, b, 3a$ and $2b = 6a + 4b$
Q4	A
	1 kilometre = 1000 metres
	1 metre = 100 centimetres
	1 centimetre = 10 millimetres
	1 kilometre = 1000 × 100 × 10 = 1 000 000 millimetres
Q5	A
	5°C − (−1°C) = 6°C
Q6	E
	The grid increases by 7 going across. X = 33 + 7 = 40
	The grid increases by 13 going down. Y = 39 + 13 = 52
Q7	E
	Five lines of symmetry

Q8	B
	25% of 32 = 32 ÷ 4 = 8 have a packed lunch
	32 − 8 = 24 have a school lunch
Q9	D
	The cube has eight vertices, the cylinder has no vertices.
Q10	C
	20 cm = 8 inches, so 200 cm = 80 inches

Test 11

Q1	C
	400 570
Q2	E
Q3	A
	2.46 kg on the scale + 0.5 kg (or 500 grams) = 2.96 kg
Q4	B
	Area of one triangle = $\frac{1}{2}$ × base × height
	= $\frac{1}{2}$ × 6 × 5 = 15 cm²
	There are three triangles. 3 × 15 cm² = 45 cm²
Q5	D
	$\frac{1}{3}$ of £36 = £36 ÷ 3 = £12
	The cost of the game in the sale is £36 − £12 = £24
	Vijay has £30
	£30 − £24 = £6 change

Q6   **B**

The right angle (90°) is a quarter of the pie chart.

$\frac{1}{4}$ of 1700 = 1700 ÷ 4 = 425

Q7   **A**

11 m + 5 m + 11 m + 5 m = 32 metres of fencing

Q8   **E**

There are 180° in a triangle. Base angles in an isosceles triangle are equal.

180° − 70° − 70° = 40°

Q9   **D**

$\frac{7}{6}$ is $\frac{1}{6}$ away from 1

None of the other fractions are as close.

Q10   **C**

Test 12

Q1   **B**

3 × **20** = 60

Q2   **D**

Q3   **C**

Six equilateral triangles fit into a regular hexagon.

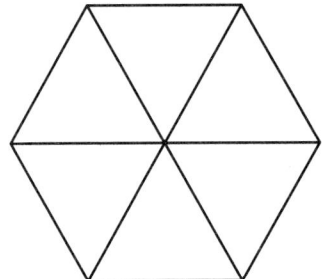

Q4   **A**

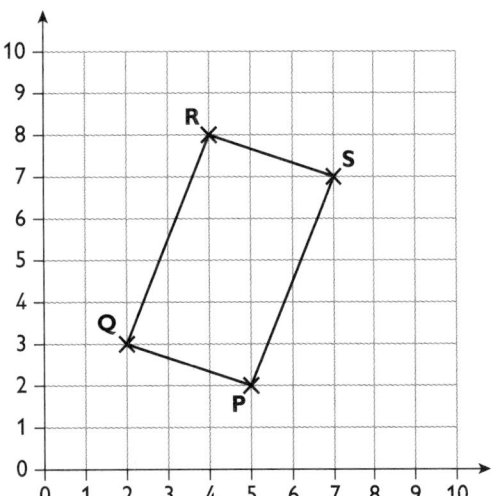

Q5   **B**

One banana costs 60p ÷ 2 = 30p

Three bananas cost 30p × 3 = 90p

Four apples cost £2.50 − 90p = £1.60

One apple costs £1.60 ÷ 4 = 40p

Five apples cost 40p × 5 = 200p = £2

Q6   **A**

24 + 38 = 62

62 − 1 = 61

38 + 61 = 99

99 − 1 = 98

Q7   **D**

$\frac{3}{5}$ of 210 = 42 × 3 = 126

25% of 126 = 126 ÷ 4 = 31.5

Q8   **E**

A is incorrect as the total is 62.

B is incorrect as 19 people ran faster than 26 minutes.

C is incorrect as 43 people ran slower than 25 minutes (half of 62 = 31).

D is incorrect as 56 people had times between 21 and 35 minutes.

E is correct as 46 people ran times faster than 31 minutes (46 > 31).

Q9   **E**

There are 360° around the clock, each hour.

360° ÷ 12 = 30°

5 × 30° = 150°

Q10   **E**

57.36 kilometres = 57 360 metres (1000 metres = 1 kilometre)

Rounded to the nearest 100 metres = 57 400 metres = 57.4 kilometres

Test 13

Q1   **D**

Q2   **E**

$\frac{3}{5}$ of 35 = 35 ÷ 5 × 3 = 21

15% of 200 = 30

$\frac{2}{3}$ of 30 = 20

75% of 24 = 18

$\frac{1}{4}$ of 68 = 17 (smallest)

Q3   **A**

There are six identical faces on a cube.

Each face has an area of 5 cm × 5 cm = 25 cm²

Total area of wood needed is 25 cm² × 6 = 150 cm²

Q4   **C**

246 ÷ 15 = 16 remainder 6 metres

Q5   **C**

87 − 23 = 64

64 ÷ 8 = 8 passengers in each carriage

Q6   **E**

2 parts = £10 (the difference between Molly's and Gigi's number of parts)

1 part = £5

Kim gets 2 × £5 = £10

Q7   **B**

Angle *a* = 90° + 45° = 135°

(the isosceles triangle has angles of 90°, 45°, 45°)

Q8   **D**

120 is divisible by both 8 and 15

Q9   **E**

In a rhombus, opposite angles are equal.

Q10   **A**

7.36 hours is 7 hours and 0.36 hours

0.36 hours = 0.36 × 60 = 21.6 minutes

0.6 minutes = 0.6 × 60 = 36 seconds

Test 14

Q1   **A**

12 + 14 × 5 = 12 + 70 = 82

Q2   **D**

5 cm + 7.2 cm + 3.7 cm + 1.9 cm + 4.6 cm = 22.4 cm

Q3   **A**

5 730 000 + 573 000 + 5730 = 6 308 730

Q4	B
	Overall, Shaun scored 6 points fewer than Amina (not 8)
Q5	B
Q6	C
	144 is 75% of the people in the cinema.
	25% = 144 ÷ 3 = 48 (number of adults)
	The total number of people = 144 + 48 = 192
Q7	E
	The length of the rectangle is 6 squares.
	12 cm ÷ 6 = 2 cm, so the squares have side length 2 cm.
	The width of the rectangle is 5 squares.
	5 × 2 cm = 10 cm
Q8	E
	0809 to 0901 is 1 minute (0810) + 50 minutes = (0900) + 1 minute (0901) = 52 minutes
Q9	D
	£0.55 × 3 = £1.65
	£2.55 – £1.65 = £0.90
	£0.90 ÷ 2 = £0.45
Q10	A
	The garden could be as short as 14.95 m (which rounds up to 15.0 to the nearest tenth).
	15.05 rounds to 15.1 to the nearest tenth.
	14.09 rounds to 14.1 to the nearest tenth.
	14.05 rounds to 14.1 to the nearest tenth.
	15.09 rounds to 15.1 to the nearest tenth.

Test 15

Q1	B
	12 + 16 = 28
	28 × 124 = 3472
Q2	B
	A pentagon has exterior angles of 72° (360° ÷ 5) and interior angles of 108° (180° – 72°).
Q3	E
	240 ÷ 5 = 48 coins
	48 × 18 mm = 864 mm = 86.4 cm
Q4	C
	The largest area that can be made is in the shape of a square.
	Each side can be 30 cm.
	30 cm × 30 cm = 900 cm^2
Q5	C
	Remember to do the multiplication first, following the correct order of operations.

6 + 7 × 8 − 5 = 57	5 + 8 × 7 − 6 = 55	**7 + 5 × 6 − 8 = 29**	8 + 7 × 6 − 5 = 45	8 + 7 × 5 − 6 = 37

Q6	E
	The square of 25 = 25 × 25 = 625
	The square of 15 = 15 × 15 = 225
	625 – 225 = 400
Q7	A
	£80 reduced by 25% = £80 – £20 = £60
	£50 reduced by 10% = £50 – £5 = £45
	£60 – £45 = £15
Q8	D
	$\frac{3}{5}$ of 20 = 20 ÷ 5 × 3 = 12
	$\frac{1}{4}$ of 20 = 20 ÷ 4 = 5
	12 + 5 = 17
	20 – 17 = 3
Q9	A
	The number 17 bus arrives at 11.35 am.
	The number 18 bus arrives at 11.40 am.
	The number 17 bus arrives first by 5 minutes.
Q10	D

Test 16

Q1	D
	420p ÷ 12 = 35p
	35p × 15 = 525p
	£5.25
Q2	A
	16 cm × 2 = 32 cm
	48 cm – 32 cm = 16 cm
	16 cm ÷ 2 = 8 cm
Q3	D
	Pat is 15 now and his sister is 5.
	In five years, he will be 20 and she will be 10.
Q4	E
	100 × 100 × 100 = 1 000 000
Q5	C
	3 octagons = 16 × 3 = 48 people
	48 plus an extra 6 (from 3 sections) = 54 people
Q6	C
	175p ÷ 100 = 1.75p per tea bag, which is the best value
Q7	A
	8 × 4 – 7 = 32 – 7 = 25
Q8	E
	–27, –20, **–13**, –6, 1
	The sequence increases by 7 each time.
Q9	D
	3000 ÷ 175 = 17 remainder 25
Q10	B

Test 17

Q1	B
	Most two-storey houses are 8 to 10 metres tall.
Q2	D
Q3	A
	North to west is 90°.
	West to south-west is 45°.
	90° + 45° = 135°
Q4	C
	120 ÷ 4 = 30 (lots of 4 litres)
	30 × 15 minutes = 450 minutes
	450 minutes = 7 hours 30 minutes = 7.5 hours
Q5	E
	Prime numbers between 20 and 30 are 23 and 29
	23 + 29 = 52
Q6	A
	75% of 152 = 114
	60% of 240 = 144
	144 – 114 = 30

Q7	**B**
	Perpendicular lines cross at right angles.
Q8	**D**
	The difference between −9°C and −1°C is 8°C
	−1°C − −9°C = −1°C + 9°C = 8°C
Q9	**B**
	48 students represent half of the pie chart.
	So there are 48 × 2 = 96 students altogether.
Q10	**E**
	Each desk needs 1.5 m.
	10 × 1.5 m = 15 m
	There will be one more desk at the end of the row, which makes 16 metres in total.

Test 18

Q1	**D**
Q2	**C**

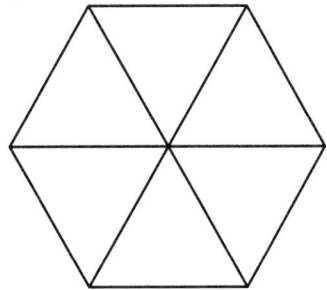

Q3	**B**
	From the graph, 8 inches is 20 cm.
	Therefore 16 inches would equal 40 cm.
Q4	**E**

Soup and Pasta   Garlic bread and Pasta   Melon and Pasta
Soup and Pizza   Garlic bread and Pizza   Melon and Pizza
Soup and Salad   Garlic bread and Salad   Melon and Salad

Q5	**C**
	£482 − £34 = £448
	£448 ÷ 2 = £224
	Joe £224 (and Jill £258)
Q6	**D**

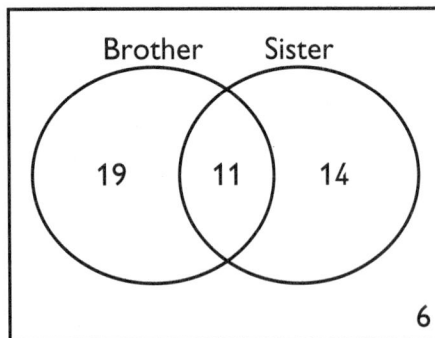

Q7	**B**
	2.5 kg = 2500 g
	1.75 kg = 1750 g
	2500 g + 1750 g + 800 g = 5050 g = 5.05 kg
Q8	**A**

	Walk	Cycle	Car or bus	Total
Girls	15	26	11	52
Boys	18	22	8	48
Total	33	48	19	100

Q9	**D**
	Six sides of 5 cm = 30 cm
Q10	**D**
	£60 represents 100% − 25% = 75%
	Therefore, 25% = £60 ÷ 3 = £20
	£60 + £20 = £80 (the original price or 100%)

Test 19

Q1	**D**
	3 hours 25 minutes = 3 × 60 minutes + 25 minutes = 205 minutes
	$1\frac{1}{4}$ hours = 60 minutes + 15 minutes = 75 minutes
	205 minutes − 75 minutes = 130 minutes = 2 hours and 10 minutes
Q2	**C**
Q3	**B**
	Perimeter = 7 cm + 4 cm + 7 cm + 3 cm + 4 cm + 7 cm + 4 cm = 36 cm
Q4	**A**
	£3.54 ÷ 3 = £1.18 per pen
	£1.18 × 7 = £8.26
Q5	**B**
	1360 ÷ 8 = 170
Q6	**C**
	The interior angles of a square equal 90° and the interior angles of an equilateral triangle equal 60°.
	Angles around a point = 360°
	x = 360° − 90° − 60° = 210°
Q7	**E**
	1 is not a prime number so A and B are incorrect.
	39 is divisible by 3 and so is not prime (C) and 15 is divisible by 3 so is not prime (D).
	Only E is correct.
Q8	**A**
	Four counters are added on each time.
	Pattern 3 has 13 counters.
	13 + 4 = 17 counters for pattern 4
Q9	**D**
	3 cm = 10 m, 6 cm = 20 m, 1.5 cm = 5 m
	7.5 cm = 20 m + 5 m = 25 m
Q10	**B**
	An isosceles triangle has two equal angles (and sides).

Test 20

Q1	**B**
	3^2 = 3 × 3 = 9
	9^2 = 9 × 9 = 81
	So the number is 3
Q2	**B**
	$2\frac{2}{3} + 3 = 5\frac{2}{3}$ and $5\frac{2}{3} + \frac{1}{3} = 6$
	$2\frac{2}{3} + 3\frac{1}{3} = 6$
Q3	**A**

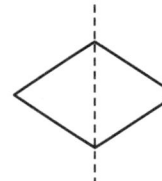

Q4   **C**

$\frac{5}{7}$ of 280 = 280 ÷ 7 × 5 = 200

200 seeds grow into flowers.

280 − 200 = 80

80 seeds do not grow into flowers.

Q5   **B**

300 ÷ 12 = 25

So 25 g of plain flour needed for each mince pie.

475 ÷ 25 = 19 mince pies can be made

Q6   **E**

From the list, only a cube has 8 vertices.

Q7   **E**

500 ÷ 35 = 14 remainder 10

14 × 35p = 490p = £4.90

£5 − £4.90 = £0.10

Q8   **B**

£20 is 80% of the original price (100% − 20% = 80%)

20% is £5 (£20 ÷ 4) so the original 100% was 5 × £5 = £25 (5 × 20% = 100%)

Q9   **D**

(0 × 7) + (1 × 8) + (2 × 12) + (3 × 4)
= 0 + 8 + 24 + 12 = 44

Q10   **A**

The large hexagon has six sides, made up of the sides of 12 equilateral triangles.

36 cm ÷ 12 = 3 cm, so each side of the equilateral triangles is 3 cm.

The shaded hexagon has the sides of six equilateral triangles.

6 × 3 cm = 18 cm

Test 21

Q1   **D**

12 × 12 = 144

0.12 × 12 = 1.44

$(0.12)^2$ = 0.12 × 0.12 = 0.0144

Q2   **B**

3.6 litres × 2 = 7.2 litres total capacity

$\frac{2}{3}$ of 7.2 litres = 7.2 litres ÷ 3 × 2 = 2.4 × 2 = 4.8 litres

4.8 litres − 3.6 litres = 1.2 litres extra required

Q3   **E**

Total interior angles in a pentagon = 540° (3 × 180°)

540° − 105° − 105° = 330°

3 × y = 330°

y = 110°

Q4   **C**

995 rounded to the nearest 10 is 1000 and any number between 1000 and 1005 rounded to the nearest 10 is 1000.

Q5   **A**

The dimensions of the open box are

10 cm − 4 cm = 6 cm, 7 cm − 4 cm = 3 cm and 2 cm.

The capacity is 6 cm × 3 cm × 2 cm = 36 cm³

Q6   **E**

Q7   **C**

2.4 × 36 = 86.4

So 2.4 × 36 000 = 86.4 × 1000 = 86 400

Q8   **D**

Q9   **D**

4000 mm = 400 cm

400 cm = 4 m

4 m = 0.004 km

Q10   **E**

The rectangle is split into eight equal parts.

$\frac{1}{8}$ = 12.5% so $\frac{3}{8}$ = 37.5%

Test 22

Q1   **B**

3.4 + 4.1 = 7.5

7.5 ÷ 2 = 3.75

Q2   **D**

−2 × −2 = 4

4 × −2 = −8

Q3   **E**

The difference between their ages is 23 years.

When Tilly is 23, Bob will be double her age (46).

Q4   **A**

63 − 56 = 7

$\frac{7}{56}$ = $\frac{1}{8}$ = 0.125 = 12.5%

Q5   **A**

Q6   **D**

(£3.40 × 3) + (£1.60 × 8) = £23.00

Q7   **B**

Each term is half the value of the previous term.

Q8   **C**

The average height of a woman is approximately 1.6 m.

The tree in the diagram is about four times the height of the woman.

4 × 1.6 m = 6.4 m

Q9   **C**

```
      6
      6
    9 9 +
   ─────
    1 1 1
```

Q10   **E**

Notes

Notes